A Jesuit's Journey
through the
Turbulent 1960s

A Jesuit's Journey
through the
Turbulent 1960s

Paul Swift

ISBN-10: 1-5170-8957-3

ISBN-13: 978-1-5170-8957-3

Questions or comments can be directed to
PaulSwiftJourney@gmail.com

The front cover photo, taken by Paul Brown, is from
the 1970 edition of *The Cage*, the yearbook of
Bellarmine Preparatory School in Tacoma,
Washington, courtesy of Fred Mayovsky, SJ.

The author portrait on the back cover
is by Nicole Swift.

Ad Majorem Dei Gloriam
And to the Memory of My Mother,
Kathleen Mary O'Reilly Swift

Contents

Foreword

When my old friend Paul Swift asked me to write the foreword to this book, I was both honored and perplexed. I have very few credits as a print writer. I do have some in TV and film, but I hardly see how those might count in the company of so many highly literate Jesuits that Paul so effortlessly brings to life in this book.

I am also no more Catholic than Jewish, though most of my lifetime friends have been either one or the other. I grew up as the only non-churchgoer in a heavily Irish Catholic neighborhood, but the best lesson I learned from that was how to do something considered socially unacceptable and get away with it. When I walked past the breezy courtyard of the Immaculate Heart of Mary towards my Protestant white-bread grade school, I can recall gawking at the girls with their cotton windblown skirts and their wooly socks consuming their calves, lined up alongside wisecracking boys in their blue blazers and strange little beanie caps. I thought that—despite all those cruel, repressive measures they endured from the Brothers and the Sisters—maybe they had more fun simply because they had something concrete to rebel against. That they might be getting a better education never occurred to me. I did know they had much better coaching on the basketball courts when it came to applying a sharp elbow to an opposing Adam's apple to steal or control the ball.

None of my old neighborhood pals would stay the course past the eighth grade, when they were freed to jaunt off to our public high school. But then, none of them were smart enough, or at least bookish enough, to even be considered for a Jesuit school. That's what I couldn't get about those Catholics. Most of their rituals and beliefs were scorned by my friends, and they made about as much sense to me as they now make to satirists like Bill Maher. And yet, as I grew older I'd find some of the most innovative, not to mentioned disciplined, people of the times were Catholic, and particularly those who were Jesuit-educated.

Two-time California Governor Jerry Brown, a former Jesuit, was certainly one. Another was an eminent Catholic philosopher, who was also my NYU Classics professor. David Leahy dazzled SRO classrooms with his impassioned analysis of classics like *The Iliad*. This he'd illustrate with Greek and Hebrew root words connected by circles and arrows that he'd furiously slap across a giant blackboard that looked like the offspring of an intricate mathematical proof and an abstract-expressionist-turned-minimalist word mural exploding from the head of Zeus. Professor Leahy would also fill the NYU auditorium by debating a topic like "What's the value of student demonstrations?" There, in the very heart of the student protest movement, he'd leave most of us stunned, and though not perhaps converted, at least questioning that value.

This was in the heyday of Greenwich Village, where, despite earning a second major in Comparative Religion at NYU, I liked to say that I majored in New York City and the 1960s. But Leahy and a few of my other more learned conservative Catholic friends (mostly from Queens, of course) had made me more skeptical—or often even dismissive—of many of the cultural and intellectual pioneers of the 60s. The books by many of them—from Paul Goodman, to Marshall McLuhan, to Norman O. Brown, and even Carl Rogers—were piled high around the cash register of the Sheridan Square Bookshop where I worked. I saw them again, and others like them, referenced as so influential to the intellectual and personal growth of Paul's brilliant older brother Jerry in a letter [See *Afterword*.] he wrote after he was dismissed from his Jesuit Order so abruptly and harshly for undocumented heresy charges on the eve of his being ordained as a priest. Jerry's letter has now opened my eyes, not only to the joys and mysteries of a Jesuit education, but also to the very rich formative nature of the '60s themselves, which I had long thought I'd lived and understood far better than I really have.

You will gratefully notice when you read this wry memoir, with its tales of a rich Jesuit ferment in the heart of the tumultuous 1960s, that Paul Swift's sentences are far better sculpted than mine. This is partially due to a lifetime of editing and actually writing, and partly because his wit has long been as sharp as an apoplectic Brother's correctional switch stick. But now I see it's also thanks to his rigorous and disciplined Jesuit education. And what makes this book most interesting to a non-believing, know-nothing layman like myself is how skillfully he merges the 'ontologies' of the Jesuit experience with the "if you remember them you weren't there" 1960s.

And, while Paul has his fun with both, he clearly demonstrates how each informed the other, particularly with the movement opposed to the Vietnam War, where he worked closely with Jesuit figures like Robert Drinan and the famed, or, to mainstream America, infamous Dan Berrigan, who did some real time in stir for things like raiding a draft-board office and burning its documents with napalm. I remember these guys as the radical and fearless kingpins of the antiwar movement, but never understood before reading this book that the passion of their convictions and their philosophic reasoning were so deeply grounded in Jesuit dialectics and principles.

For many of us who lived through it, whether we are believers or non-believers, the past half-century is bookended between Pope John XXIII's "opening the Church's window" to let some sunshine in, and the current Pope Francis's restoration of a Catholic mission based more on the actual teachings of Jesus than on conservative medieval Church dogma. In the reign of the pontiffs and their appointed cardinals in between, much of how we had come to view Church dogma had to do with sexual repressiveness, child sex abuse scandals, and the defense of property rights over liberation theology and its concerns for the poor, for nature, and for our planet. Now Francis has, in words and deeds, stunned the worlds of conservatives and liberals, believers and non-believers with his denunciations of profit-making as a sole value, with its threats to all forms of life on earth, particularly the earth's growing multitudes of human beings living in poverty.

With such a radical change of perspective now emanating from the Vatican, it's easy to understand why my friend Swift, now a *mostly* matured husband and father—and a still pugnaciously witted dude— was inspired to write this warm and insightful historical memoir. After all, Francis is the first Jesuit pope in Church history. Anyone who might wonder why that's so significant is sure to get a clearer understanding in these pages. And beyond that, a better understanding of coming of age in the 1960s, an era almost as tumultuous, confounding, and yet strangely endearing as the Catholic Church and all of its offspring—including those old rebellious, wisecracking Irish American pals of mine from the realm of the Immaculate Heart of Mary.

Mark Durand
Independent TV & Film Producer and Writer
Red Hook, New York
July 2015

Acknowledgments

The remarkable Robert R. Rahl transformed my relatively shapeless manuscript into this book. I cannot thank him enough. Robert's son Jeremy Rahl designed the cover, which features a photo by Paul Brown of me in a Vietnam-era peace march, retrieved from the Bellarmine Prep (Tacoma) archives by Frederick Mayovsky, SJ. My portrait on the back cover is by my daughter Nicole Swift. Roger Guettinger helpfully provided the text of my brother Jerry's letter, which comprises the Afterword. I offer heartfelt thanks to all of them. I am also in debt to the many Jesuits who left me with lifelong memories of their dedication and visionary work.

—PS

I

Introibo ad altare Dei

Like hundreds of young Jesuits before me, who were gripped with varying degrees of devotion, battiness and resolve, I spent my first three years on a hilltop surrounded by farms and ranches. They led from the Novitiate down to the lumber-mill town of Sheridan, Oregon. In the morning, smoke plumes broke through the Yamhill Valley mist. In the evening, the lonely whistle of a freight train winding through the valley brought back vivid memories of my year and a half as a young vagabond, before I entered the Jesuits.

That was the rub, at least as far as the Novice Master was concerned. Almost all of Father Franz Mueller's charges were fresh out of high school or a year or two of college. As for me, I had spent two semesters at Marquette University, and then I hitch-hiked around Europe and into the Middle East. The spring before I entered the Jesuits, I lived in San Francisco's bohemian North Beach, after the beatniks and before the hippies.

Novice Master Mueller didn't have a large vocabulary, which might have suited his position. He often used the words *wont* and *propensity*. "Brother Swift, you are *wont* to attract followers." Another time, he told me I had a *propensity* for "humor, worldly humor." The methodical German set out to prune me, as if I were a wild bush or what the insurance adjustors call an attractive nuisance.

Father Mueller's pruning began with both private and communal spiritual exhortations to embrace humility and obedience. He also snipped his shears doling out duties and positions. His assignments for the afternoon hour of work made us all anxious. It would be a job that would last for months. Buff the chapel floors under the watch of stained-glass saints? Clean the bakery? Help Brother Bennett in the infirmary? Stir Honey Pot, the homemade tank of excremental transformations? Run the huge laundry machines? Slop pigs? Bale hay?

Father Mueller gave me the only solo job. He appointed me the bookbinder. Like Rapunzel, I spent months in a tower. Instead of long flowing hair, I had three glue pots. From my tower, I looked down at the oak forests and farm fields dotted with my toiling brothers. I began work by warming the pots to the required temperatures. While I stirred the glue, I lined up the day's books to be resuscitated. They were hardcover hymnals, textbooks and lives of the saints. I took pride in my work, because the finished products would be used throughout the Novitiate.

The only visitor I ever received in my workshop was Father Fredric Schlatter. He was the urbane Academic Dean, Librarian and Professor of Classics. He entrusted me with volumes of increasing value as I improved my bookbinding skills. It was the beginning of a fruitful relationship, which lasted throughout my Jesuit career.

Irish Eyes

Two Sheridan priests I fondly remember were opposites. Father Mike McHugh was the Rector of the entire community. That included the two-year

Novitiate and the two-year Juniorate, probably about seventy-five of us, plus the faculty. Father McHugh was a big, gregarious Irishman. He was both firm and funny. One Saturday, he was kneeling in the garden near the main entrance of the imposing building, pulling weeds in his scruffs. Two nervous parents visiting their son approached him. The husband warily asked him what the Rector was like.

"You could never meet a finer man. Your son is blessed to have him as his Rector!" The couple attended Mass the next morning, only to see the "gardener" at the altar in full priestly vestments as the Rector.

Father Cornelius Mullen (Connie to his colleagues) was a brainy cherub. He taught us a more elementary Latin (Cicero and Caesar) than Father Schlatter's Ovid, Augustine and Virgil. Father Mullen's first-floor front room was large, but it was furnished with only a single bed, a kneeler, two chairs, his vow crucifix on the wall, a big desk holding a half dozen books and an ashtray full of straight Camel butts. When Father Mullen returned our Latin translations in class, each page was carefully redlined with a dizzying number of corrections.

"Father Mullen, I did my best."

He invariably replied, "Angels can do no more."

Novice Master Mueller liberated me from the monotony of novice life by naming me one of two "drivers." The droll Brother Mauer was the Novitiate's main driver. He picked up recruits at the Greyhound bus stop in Sheridan and took back the young men who had washed out of the Jesuit life. Brother Mauer plied an American Catholic River Styx.

My driving jobs were happier. I drove priests to doctors' and dentists' appointments in McMinnville and even Portland. I drove Brother Painter through the Willamette Valley to a cloistered convent in southern Oregon. The pious and polite Sister Superior bent a rule to let Brother Painter witness a dear friend taking her vows. We were all dressed in black and white, and we were all dedicated and devotional, and I carried the only driver's license.

Ignatius Loyola, the founder of the religious order that he named the Company of Jesus, was a former soldier. Many of the practices of Jesuit daily life have a military efficiency. *The Book of Common Rules* carries only twenty-four. One of them had Father Rector Michael McHugh pulling weeds on Saturday afternoon. "Spend one hour outside each day." Father Thomas Steele assigned himself the task of eradicating tansy ragweed from the premises. The only time we novices ever saw him, aside from at the head table in the refectory, was when we walked by him digging and pulling the ubiquitous invader.

Age quod agis. Do what you're doing.

The high school athletes among us played fierce basketball and soccer. They burned away energy built up in bare and celibate cubicles whose walls were so thin, the joke went, that you could hear your neighbor change his mind.

Others of us took long walks. We dressed in army surplus and second-hand denim and tramped through farms up into the hills. We often hiked past a white-fenced, green field of Black Angus cattle. We climbed deeper through the woods to High Falls or Spirit Mountain. One time we secured an all-day pass. We packed lunches and hiked across the Yamhill Valley. After climbing to the top of Dorn Peak, we celebrated as if Sir Edmund Hillary were cracking open the champagne.

Unlike the competitive sports, hiking gave us the chance to talk with one another. We came from all over the Pacific Northwest: Yakima, Missoula, Butte, Tacoma, Spokane, Portland and farm towns in between. My brother Jerry, who was eight years ahead of me in the Jesuits, had taught a few of my new comrades at Seattle Prep.

Brother Codd liked to talk about the Blessed Virgin Mary. The rest of us traded stories about our childhoods. Brother Gary LaFlam had excellent recall and an eye for detail. Listening to him taught me how to shape a story out of a fleeting incident. More important, he demonstrated that each of us had moments worth recapturing around a campfire, or on a hike. Brother LaFlam also taught me an appreciation of classical music. The music room we frequented had scores of vinyl albums, three easy chairs and fine acoustics. I especially enjoyed Dmitri Shostakovich.

The New Jerusalem

September 8 is the Feast of the Birth of Mary, nine liturgical months after the December 8 Feast of the Immaculate Conception. It is also Vow Day. The class ahead of us knelt in our beautiful chapel and professed their vows. Brother Rothrock was among them. He and I had clinked wine glasses in Paris about becoming Jesuits. Now he was David Rothrock, SJ.

Brother Fred Mayovsky became the new bookbinder. I broke him in. During the next few months, I spent the afternoon work period constructing a wood and plaster scale model of the Old City of Jerusalem, the city Jesus worked. The enterprise could not have been more different from bookbinding. The carpentry shop was a social center. Brother Jake Morton showed me the various tools and how to use the saws. Other brothers would occasionally help me out. I put them to work carving buildings and painting them white. The project became a mild curiosity all over the hilltop.

I started with a nine-square-foot frame of solid two-by-six lumber. From the plywood bottom, I formed chicken wire and plaster into the contours of the hilly city and its environs. I took it as far as the Garden of Gethsemane, which was outside the City Walls and across a valley.

I had maps and brochures from my own visit to Jerusalem two years earlier. I was a stickler for detail. My helpers made dozens of white buildings to line the labyrinthine alleys. I made sure the larger historic and religious structures mirrored reality, a reality that gave birth to myth.

2

Pope John XXIII's Open Window

In the early 1960s, American Catholicism was at its zenith. A Catholic president was in the Oval Office. Seminaries, novitiates and convents enrolled record numbers of young people. We were all intent on becoming educators, missionaries, nurses, pastors, or writers.

In 1958, a dark horse from Venice was elected Pope. The College of Cardinals picked Angelo Roncalli on the eleventh vote. The seventy-seven-year-old would bring a pastoral breath of fresh air after Pope Pius XII's rather wooden and political nineteen-year reign. Some Vatican observers dubbed the aging new pope a "stop gap."

The College of Cardinals got more than they bargained for. The new pope began rewriting Church history on his first day. He took the name of a despised anti-pope, whom everyone wanted stricken from the books. Pope John XXIII did exactly that. He appropriated the anti-pope's name. He also convened the first Vatican Council in almost one hundred years, and only the second Ecumenical Council in hundreds of years. Pope John XXIII announced that he wanted to "open a window."

In his fresh-air campaign, John opened many windows to religious adversaries. For the previous one hundred years, the Roman Catholic Church had aggressively defended its claim as "The One True Church." At the First Vatican Council in 1870, the College of Cardinals declared that the Pope was "infallible in matters of faith and morals." In the 1950s, Pope Pius XII played that two-of-clubs trump card by instituting the Feast of the Assumption. It was a celebration and affirmation of the zany notion that the Virgin Mary was assumed *soul and body* into heaven. Take that, you Anglicans, who are so lukewarm to devotion to the Blessed Virgin! (The closest I've ever heard of an "assumption" actually occurring was Timothy Leary's having his ashes thrown out of a rocket into outer space.)

Pope John embraced his equally rotund and open-minded counterpart in the Church of England, the Archbishop of Canterbury. John also met with Jewish leaders and elders. He knew many of them from his days as Apostolic Delegate to Turkey, Greece and Bulgaria before and during the War. He had harbored entire congregations and secured safe passage for many individuals. John's initiatives gave birth to the Ecumenical Movement.

Pope John also threw a few things *out* of the Church window. The Latin Mass for starters. Then he turned the altar around, literally. Over the centuries, the celebration of Mass had become a rite of worship. A heavily garbed priest offered sacrifice to God on behalf of the congregation behind him. By having the altar face the people, John re-capitulated the original Eucharist, the Last Supper. The priest faced the people when he held up the chalice of wine and the paten of bread and repeated Jesus' words, "This is my body which is given for you."

Pope John exhorted his bishops and pastors to remember that the *people* are the Church. "We are their servants, not the other way around." He was the first (and last) modern pope to walk the streets of Rome. The Italians liked his mingling with them so much they nicknamed him Johnnie Walker, after the Scotch whisky. Here's a quick look at his wit. He was escorting a group of well-heeled American Catholic women through the Vatican. One of them asked him, "Your Holiness, just how many people work in the Vatican?"

Pope John replied, "About half."

That civic and religious euphoria began to wane one day in November 1963. That morning, I walked through the silent and empty foyer toward the chapel for the Angelus. The small bulletin board outside the chapel caught my eye. It always posted only one 3 x 5 card: "Mass 6:20." Now there was an additional card. I walked over and read it: "President Kennedy was shot today, in a motorcade in Dallas, and is not expected to live. Please keep him in your prayers."

My prayers? Sure, I'll keep him in my prayers. What else do I have to do but keep Kennedy, shot on a downtown freeway, in my prayers?

Shortly after President Kennedy's murder, the Novitiate had the first big parents' weekend of the fall. Families arrived loaded with newspaper and magazine photographs, which none of us had ever seen. They luridly documented the assassination and its aftermath. The color photographs and out-sized headlines moved me far less than the two sentences typed on a 3 x 5 card. Our country was crossing a burning bridge, with Jackie's pink dress and pillbox hat on the far bank.

Living a monastic life did not make me an informed voter in the 1964 Presidential election. At Marquette University, I had read Senator Barry Goldwater's *Conscience of a Conservative* and wrote a paper on it. His campaign for "open shops" appealed to me, because I thought no one should be forced to join a union.

During the campaign, President Johnson's people spread the word that if you voted for Goldwater, the Vietnam War would escalate. I did, and it did.

Come September 1965, I took the perpetual vows of poverty, chastity and obedience, not those weak-tea promises that diocesan priests and Protestant ministers make. On his congratulatory holy card, Novice Master Mueller wrote, "You have tramped a long road and sacrificed generously to arrive at this day."

My vows not only liberated me from the strict novice life, they also coincided with Pope John XXIII's liberalization of the Church. Mass became happier. We hosted a group of Lutheran divinity students from Salem to share a service in our chapel. The new Father Minister, who ran our material lives, introduced beer parties and encouraged long weekend trips to our ramshackle complex on the Oregon Coast. I drove Brother Fenton Melia down to a fish shack in a small harbor, where he carefully chose huge salmons to grill.

Brother LaFlam secured two-reel, black-and-white art films made in France or Italy for our viewing pleasure and education.

One Saturday evening, Gary and I were the two finalists in a Scrabble tournament. We were three points apart and each of us had four tiles. I told him I could go out and win, but it wasn't my turn. "I can go out too," Gary said, "but I don't think my word is in the book." In the stifling novitiate atmosphere, Gary's play took intellectual derring-do. *Merriam-*

Webster's Collegiate didn't list the word *turd*. I would have split my winnings with him if there had been any.

The studies were intensive. A grade of B- was the best I could muster in Father Schlatter's Latin class. ("Brother Swift, please define the future passive periphrastic.") French came easier because I took it in college and had lived in France. The jolly Father Olivier, fresh from San Francisco State University, brought a contagious enthusiasm to English lit. A few of us even signed up for German. Years later in New York City, I was dismayed to realize I had studied Greek, Latin, French and German, and had majored in English, only to come up short on the Spanish that my Puerto Rican neighbors were speaking.

Father Schlatter's Library

Father Schlatter's third-floor library was a bibliophile's paradise. It was both physically and intellectually open. Aisles of wooden bookshelves led to large windows overlooking the Yamhill Valley. Polished tables and display cases held the liberal *National Catholic Reporter, The New York Times Magazine*, the intelligent Jesuit magazine *America*, and a number of other literate Catholic publications. Some of them featured the prize-winning poet Daniel Berrigan, SJ. His writings first made me question our military presence in Vietnam. During that time I received postcards from former fellow novices from Army boot camp. Two of those friends would return from Vietnam in body bags.

I thumbed through the library's collection of Greek and Roman classics and English and American literature. If there were any mathematical or scientific titles, I didn't notice. The library also housed a modest collection of rare books and first editions.

Years later, I read that James Joyce's family in Ireland was close to the D'Arcy family. The Joyce clan gave the D'Arcy clan a few first editions of *Ulysses*. The D'Arcy name jumped off the page! The educated and affluent D'Arcy family of Salem, Oregon, had donated our beautiful chapel of St. Barbara.

The D'Arcy family also donated an original edition of *Ulysses*. Father Schlatter told me about his most prized library holding. D'Arcy family members had slipped the "pornographic" novel out of Ireland, carried it in a satchel across Canada, and unlawfully brought it into the United States. Consider the contradictions: The anti-clerical James Joyce's most acclaimed work is illegally housed in an obscure Jesuit library.

A more recent addition to the library was less noteworthy. The four-by-six-foot, stand-alone bulletin board framed in a polished wood was handsome and practical. Scholastics two years ahead of me had built it. I told Father Schlatter there was only one thing wrong with the bulletin board. "It's empty. There's nothing on it."

He replied, "I can remember ordering it to be built, but I cannot remember why."

I proposed that I mount a series of exhibits of the Impressionist and post-Impressionist painters. He asked me where I'd get the materials. He admitted the library was weak in that regard. I replied, "The Portland Public Library."

"Need I remind you, Brother Swift, that the aforementioned library is in Portland?"

"I'm a house driver."

Father Schlatter smiled. He agreed to what became the bulletin board's educational and enjoyable maiden voyage.

My drives to the huge Georgian Revival Central Library in Portland sure beat parsing scruples to an icy confessor on the hilltop. My library card (aided by my Roman collar) was a passport to the Paris I had loved and lived in. The gracious young women lent me matted prints of Cézanne, Manet, Monet, Picasso and van Gogh, among others. (Renoir found no room on my bulletin board.) On one of the few typewriters available on the hilltop, I wrote descriptions of the paintings, the artists and their techniques. The Impressionists threw representational and religious art to the haystacks.

I spent many hours in the library. Aside from typing and posting my "corkboard seminars," I wrote a short story. "A Sketch of San Francisco" featured two hours in the life of a Chinatown bum. His lack of possessions and his care for the pigeons mirrored those of the city's patron saint.

"Paul," Father Schlatter said to me one afternoon. "You spend so much time here that I am going to have to start charging you rent."

"Father, we both have taken a vow of poverty. I can't give you what I don't have, and you can't accept what you're not allowed to have."

"Nicely put. If only your Latin were as good as your English. Your rent is over there." He pointed to an expensive side table under an oil painting of Francis Xavier.

"You want me to move it?"

"No, that is its home. I want you to strip it and refinish it. I saw you working with wood on your model of Jerusalem."

"Father, there's a big difference between pine lumber and . . . mahogany?"

"Good eye, Paul. And the inlay is hard maple."

"*Ergo?*"

He explained that the library's newest donation was not marred or chipped, but it was coated with layers of oil, lacquer and wax. Even the strip of minute filigree, which framed the mirror-smooth top surface, was encrusted. How could I say no to Father Schlatter? It also looked like a better gig than extricating poison-oak vines from the trunks of scrub oak trees.

For all the hours I gave to that side table, I could have constructed a scale model of the entire Holy Land, plus the cedars of Lebanon to the north and the Red Sea to the south. I stripped the table and its four legs with three applications and removals. I couldn't use strong chemicals or strong brushes. Or haste. The rectangular band of delicate intricacies demanded a Zen-like patience and attention to detail. I applied a mild alcohol and worked it into the tiny crevices with a brush so soft you could brush a toddler's first tooth with it. The wood responded because it wasn't veneer.

Finally, I announced to Father Schlatter that I had returned the table to its birthday suit. I stripped it clean. He was very pleased. He rewarded me with three bottles of clear lacquer. "You are halfway home." He was right. The refinishing took as much time as the stripping. I brushed on numerous coats. I smoothed each application with very, very fine sand paper. I was careful not to leave even the faintest line. The rich wood drank up the lacquer, except the top surface. It was as smooth as marble but lacked marble's porosity.

It's too late to make a long story short, but let me try. Father Schlatter gave me the address of an antique dealer in McMinnville. I drove there and bought an eye-drop additive to eliminate the tabletop's miniscule "fish bubbles." Coupled with a brush as fine as an angel's pubic hair, the additive smoothed my way to a successful conclusion. Saint Francis Xavier and Father Fredric Schlatter both blessed me.

Priests from all walks of Jesuit life stayed for a while at the St. Francis Xavier Novitiate for various reasons. In my third year, Brother Bennett, RN, told me he had a new resident in the infirmary. He said I'd like him. Father Phil Soreghan's left arm was limp after a stroke. "Are you right-handed?" I asked him.

"I am now," he laughed.

Three or four evenings a week I rubbed his bad arm. He liked my massaging his hand—the palm, the fingers. "The fingers, Paul, I miss the fingers most."

"Were you a piano player?"

He smiled. "No. I just liked tapping them across my temple to make people think I was thinking."

Father Phil spent his life at Seattle University as a popular theology professor and marriage counselor. He dispelled the notion that a priest couldn't have anything to say about being married. His talent was common sense. One evening, I confided to him that, even though I had just professed my perpetual vows, I was thinking of leaving the Order. Father Phil didn't miss a beat. "Paul, get yourself a large woman. She's good heat in the winter and good shade in the summer."

The less edifying Richard J. O'Dea, SJ, also spent a few weeks at the Novitiate. He and I had crossed paths (and swords) when I was a junior at Gonzaga Preparatory School. Father O'Dea replaced the longtime and popular Principal, Father Gordon Toner. The two couldn't have been more different. Father O'Dea had spent time in Ireland and wanted to introduce Irish boarding-school discipline to Gonzaga Prep. The higher-ups nixed his plan for blazers and neckties. He autocratically ran the Student Council meetings, which technically were supposed to be conducted by the Student Body President.

During one of his daily Principal's briefings over the PA system, Father O'Dea announced a new policy. "It was voted in by the Student Council."

"The hell it was," I blurted out loud to the whole classroom. "It was shoved down our throats." Mister Blanchette, who was usually uneasy in front of fifteen teenage boys, rose to the occasion. "Paul, we are going to the Principal's office, where you will repeat to him what you just said. And don't leave out the swearing, 'The *hell* it was.'"

I welcomed the opportunity to tell Father O'Dea my opinion. I repeated my outburst. Father O'Dea promptly expelled me from Gonzaga Prep. No questions asked. Case closed.

My mother was devastated. She and I had a sacrificed a lot to come up with the $180 tuition each year, and she respected the Jesuit education. As a legal secretary, she also knew a thing or two about influence. She called my brother Jerry, who was in his third year at St. Francis Xavier Novitiate. She told him to "get things straightened out." The resolution put Father O'Dea's admitting he had overreacted and my apologizing for swearing.

The following year Father O'Dea and I exchanged places. He was removed from Gonzaga Prep, and I was running Student Council meetings as Student Body President. I was elected partly because my confrontation with Father O'Dea had made me a working-class hero.

Now I was a squeaky clean new Jesuit, and Father O'Dea was cooling his heels (and a more problematic body part at the other end of his legs) on the hilltop. The tall, dark and handsome priest had fallen in love with a woman while in graduate school at LSU. Father Mike McHugh, his classmate and old friend, was helping Father O'Dea get his priestly life back in order. I was tempted to greet him, "How the hell is it going?"

3

Ontology Recapitulates Monotony

The Society of Jesus followed Pope John's relaxation of the old traditions. The Jesuits began moving their scholastics from hilltops to their own college campuses. My class and the one ahead of us moved from Sheridan *en masse* (including Brother Bennett and Father Soreghan) to Mount St. Michael's School of Philosophy. It overlooked my hometown of Spokane and it was an easy drive to Gonzaga University.

Father Thomas O'Keefe, a Canadian Jesuit, introduced us to philosophy by endlessly running steel balls through his fingers, like the nervous Captain Queeg, and then setting one or two of them on his desk. Ontology is the study of existence. What exists between those balls?

Our studies intensified and diversified. All of us were required to major in Philosophy in addition to our own major of choice. My Gonzaga University diploma two years later hid the fact that I had earned exactly twice the 128 credits required. My 256 degrees met the requirements for two majors (Philosophy and English) and two minors. I should have been given *two* diplomas, but I wasn't alone at the all-you-can-eat academic buffet.

Tony Gasperino, for example, was a biologist at heart. He majored in the obligatory Philosophy as well as his beloved English Literature. (He played a bawdy Falstaff in our production of *Henry IV*.) After Tony left the Jesuits, as most of us eventually did, Battelle Industries scooped him up. He was a literate biologist equally at home with the microscope and the typewriter.

The Mount St. Michael's student body was also more diverse. In an attempt to make the Jesuit Provinces less provincial, a small number of scholastics were shifted to other Provinces to study philosophy. The Mount received a dozen from the English-speaking Canadian Province and more than twenty from the California Province.

Once again, my position as house driver served me well. I picked up many of these immigrants at the airport. Being their first contact made me their point man for two years. One day, for example, two scholastics from India got a flat tire down in Spokane. Over the telephone, I barely understood Rudy's high-pitched Raj English: "We've ponctured a pneumatic and don't know how to open the boot." Two scholastics from Malta also befriended me. They peppered me with questions about life in America. I showed them America by taking them to my parents' home. My father pulled out an album of his mounted and illustrated postage stamps titled "Malta."

The move from an all-male hilltop to classes with laymen and lay-able women presented me with the horniest summer of my life. Reading John Updike's *The Centaur* didn't help. I read more than I prayed. I studied German. I took breaks from the campus's sultry distractions in the second floor of the Crosby Library. The first floor foyer displayed Gold Records awarded to Gonzaga's most famous alumnus and generous benefactor, Bing Crosby. The second floor displayed the side table I had stripped and refinished. It stood between shelved books transplanted from the St. Francis Xavier Juniorate library. Father Schlatter presided over this library reserved for us Jesuit scholastics.

My good friend from high school and summers working on a cattle ranch, Mike Meighan, met me on campus one afternoon. We walked along the Spokane River, saying our goodbyes. He was leaving for two years as a Peace Corps volunteer in Niger. That experience and the friends he made among his fellow volunteers stayed with him the rest of his life—much like my years as a Jesuit.

The transition from the Middle Ages to the Modern Age was just that, a transition. We scholastics took our first-year philosophy courses at Mount St. Michael's. The Systems track meant ontology and epistemology. The History track gave us the Ancient Greeks and the Middle Ages, dominated by Thomistic Scholasticism.

We attended the rest of our classes at Gonzaga University. I took a course in Faulkner and Hemingway. Their only thing in common was a nationality. The professor told us how to read William Faulkner. "Pour yourself a snifter of brandy, relax in an easy chair and enjoy his mastery of the language and a culture. *The Sound and the Fury* will be due by next class." *Enjoy* 675 pages of complex prose in two days?

After seventeen years as President of Seattle University, The Reverend A. A. "Arby" Lemieux was named Rector of Mount St. Michael's. It was a masterful appointment. During the booming post-war years, Father Lemieux transformed the college into a university. By enlisting the Seattle business community, including his friend Bill Boeing, he put

Seattle University on the national map. Arby Lemieux also made it a point to get to know the students. At ten every morning, he hung around the student union, and his office door was always open.

He was only too happy that his new student body was the next generation of Jesuits. He spent a lot of leisure time with us. He went golfing with the sons of the country club set. He once took some of them on a golfing excursion to the Canadian Rockies. When he was asked to give the Commencement Address at the nearby Whitworth College, he enlisted three of us to write it. "Make it contemporary. Quote Bob Dylan, maybe Janis Joplin. No, not Miss Joplin. These graduates are Presbyterians."

"How about Reinhold Niebuhr?" John Barrett-Hamilton from Winnipeg suggested.

During those halcyon days of American Catholicism, the celebration of the Mass became, well, a *Celebration!* All across America, priests like Father Lemieux celebrated Mass facing the people. His fellow priests spread their arms wide to embrace the entire congregation. Convents of nuns flew out of Pope John's open window like papal doves, or pigeons. Many of them crapped all over Mass with guitars and folk music and vapid sing-alongs. My brother Jerry told me he once harbored an un-Christian thought as he stood in line for Holy Communion. The nun in front of him raised her song page to his face and scolded him for not singing. Jerry went to a public rather than a parochial grade school, and he never did have much use for nuns.

Mount St. Michael's was famous for its choir. When Jerry was at the Mount, he got our mother and me tickets to Midnight Mass. The chapel was packed with Spokane's Catholic elite. From the loft above and behind us, the male choir filled the chapel with harmony, Gregorian chant and medieval ballads celebrating Jesus' birth.

Jerry Swift and Terry Shea had done a lot together since they became friends at Gonzaga Prep. They produced the senior yearbook. Their team won the State debate championship. Possibly, their most enduring and endearing collaboration was *A Christmas Symphony*. This pair of twenty-four-year-old Jesuit scholastics harnessed the beauty of the Mount St. Michael's choir into a long-play album. Terry and Jerry were both well versed in Classical music and the Gregorian chant. Terry was the choir director and became the project director for the album. Jerry, the veteran elocutionist, had the best voice at the Mount, but he couldn't sing. He wrote and narrated the program.

Terry cajoled a radio station to record the choir in the acoustically amenable chapel at Sacred Heart Hospital. Terry also cajoled Spokane's leading department store, The Crescent, to sell *A Christmas Symphony*. Spokane Catholics lapped it up for years to come.

My generation of Mount St. Michael's musicians abandoned the choir loft and the pipe organ. They took a wide space behind the last pew in the chapel. Father Lemieux heartily blessed a rock and roll band to accompany the celebration of the Mass. They were four crazy Canadians (lead guitar, bass guitar, keyboard and a full set of drums) and a vocalist from Missoula. During one memorable Sunday High Mass, a phalanx of priestly celebrants held their collective breath at the Gloria. Then they smiled. The band wailed out the popular rock song "Gloria"—as in G-L-O-R-I-A!

The aptly named Soul Concern became the most popular band on the Gonzaga University campus.

They looked professional on the raised stage, thanks to a theater major intent on learning lighting. What went through the minds of Catholic coed groupies whose rock idols wore Roman collars?

That winter a few of us organized the biggest Christmas party in the history of Mount St. Michael's. We set out to give a present to every one of the 125 priests, brothers and scholastics in residence. The project naturally attracted a number of Santa's helpers. Our budget of twenty-five dollars went mainly to wrapping paper and ribbon. We scrounged through storage rooms, outbuildings and barns. Many of the gifts were gags. For David Bruce Countryman, an ascetic who rarely bathed, we wrapped a big red ribbon around a bathtub. From a dusty manikin in a barn, I retrieved and wrapped a left arm for Father Phil Soreghan.

In another barn, we uncovered bales of Army surplus long underwear, both tops and bottoms. Father Minister, who ruled the barns and its contents, gave me the okay to take them to the Gospel Mission down on skid road. The pastors gratefully received something with which to warm their winos.

On the night of the Christmas party, jolly Father Olivier donned a red suit, which needed no padding, to play Jolly St. Nick. The Soul Concern rocked all around the Christmas tree. The band dedicated a song to Father Clifford Kossel, our dour Academic Dean. He smiled faintly when they sang Simon and Garfunkel's "I Am a Rock." I raised an eggnog toast to our beloved Rector, Arby Lemieux. "For those of you not up on your French, 'Lemieux' means 'The Best.'"

"A Re-founder of the Society"

Padre Pedro Arrupe was another bright Jesuit star who blinded me to the reactionary forces at work in the Catholic Church. He was elected Superior General of the Jesuits the same year I took my vows. He was only the second Basque to hold that high office since the founder of the Society of Jesus.

The young Pedro Arrupe studied medicine in Bilbao before entering the Jesuits at age twenty. In 1932, when the Leftists started destroying monasteries, convents and churches and outlawing religious orders, Arrupe and a few fellow Jesuits escaped to the Netherlands and Belgium. After his ordination as a priest, he went to the United States. He earned a Doctorate in Medical Ethics. From there, he was sent to Japan as a missionary.

Like his fellow Basque Jesuit, Francis Xavier, Pedro Arrupe found work in Japan discouraging. Neither of them could break through the cultural differences. During World War II, the Japanese imprisoned Arrupe on suspicion of espionage. A year later, on Christmas Eve, a loud crowd gathered outside his cell. He prayerfully faced the fact that he was going to be executed. Not so! The people were his parishioners who came to sing him Christmas carols. His jailers had a similar respect for this peaceful and polite prisoner. They eventually freed him without a trial.

The rejuvenated Father Arrupe and seven Jesuit colleagues were living in Hiroshima when the United States dropped the atomic bomb that obliterated the city. They were within the "blast zone," but survived because they were on the outskirts of town. The chapel floor was soon covered with twisting and writhing bodies. The Novitiate became a hospital. I doubt that Father Arrupe's graduate studies in Medical Ethics had a course on frying 160,000 people. But he knew enough medicine to minister to the suffering survivors.

Father Arrupe remained in Japan after the War and was appointed head of the Jesuit Province of Japan in 1955. Ten years later he was elected Superior General of the Society of Jesus. He immediately appointed the liberal, well-spoken and popular president of Fordham University, Father Vincent O'Keefe, as one of his four Assistants.

Father O'Keefe described Father General Arrupe as "a second Ignatius of Loyola, a re-founder of the Society in light of Vatican II."

In late March 1967, Father Lemieux called me into his office. "Paul, I want to be the first one to tell you, even though I find it difficult. Phil Soreghan died this morning."

After a slow, deep breath, I said, "He was a good man. He left the world a better place than he found it."

"You are right, Paul. We spent many years together at Seattle University. And now I am privileged to have lived with him here."

"I'm sure you two had a lot to talk about, and laugh about."

"Paul, I want to offer you first refusal on any part you want to play in Phil's funeral. You two were good friends."

"You mean I can say the Requiem Mass?"

"We don't have six years to wait."

I considered the options. Serve as chief acolyte. Bear the four-foot, gilded candlestick. Swing the ornate incense thurible. Maybe give the farewell homily. "Father, how about if I toll the bells during the procession to the cemetery?"

"I think Phil would like you to do that."

From the brick bell tower, I watched the funeral assembly leave the front entrance and proceed down the main drive to a shaded knoll. I matched the solemn pace with slow pulls on the heavy rope. I started to cry, but the sound of the bells reminded me of the slow conversations I enjoyed with Father Phil.

———————

At a summer cruise party on Coeur d'Alene Lake, Father Lemieux came up to me. "Paul, could you tell me what time it is?"

"Father, I haven't worn a watch since I ruined mine swimming in a Paris fountain."

"Well, you'll need one now, because I'm making you Beadle."

I was dumbfounded. Beadle is a word from olden days when it meant a minor parish functionary or college professor's assistant. At Mount St. Michael's, it was the equivalent of Student Body President. The Beadle oversaw events and outings. He posted daily instructions and emceed ceremonies and parties. He also served as a liaison between the scholastics and the faculty and administration.

My first assignment could not have been more pleasant. The Rector, the Bishop of Spokane and I presided over the dedication of a new athletic facility at Mount St. Michael's. The former university president never saw a construction site he didn't like. A swimmer himself, Father Lemieux was dismayed to see our decrepit outdoor swimming pool. He hired (or twisted the arms of) an architectural firm. Building materials were either donated or purchased at cost. For Father Lemieux, this was peanuts compared to Seattle University.

The Four Brothers, a construction team of Jesuit Brothers who had moved with us from Oregon, built the indoor swimming pool, basketball court and locker rooms.

Bernard Topel had been Bishop of Spokane for more than twenty years. Before that, the Bozeman native had earned a Master's in mathematics from the University of Notre Dame and a Doctorate from the Catholic University. He worked in a number of rural parishes in Montana. He was teaching math at Notre Dame when he was named Bishop. Instead of moving into the Bishop's Manor, he took up residence in a modest house in the lower-middle class neighborhood where I grew up. He also sold his gold crosier, gave the money to the poor and used a wooden shepherd's staff. (Years later, I learned that he attended every session of the Second Vatican Council.)

I turned to him before the dedication ceremonies began. "At the risk of being irreverent, Your Excellency. We were a dog and pony show once before."

He laughed. "Which was I?"

"Do you remember the dedication of the St. Joseph Shrine at Gonzaga Prep? As Student Body President, I introduced you."

"Yes, I remember. It was raining and someone put a plastic bag over the microphone. We had a good time."

"Permit me to jog your memory back four years earlier."

The Bishop glanced around at the spacious and bright building and the religious and lay people still filing in. "It looks like I am your hostage."

In 1956, when I was in the eighth grade, the Sacred Heart Parish Pastor John Coleman was promoted to Monsignor. Sister Bernadette Mary, our teacher, wrote and directed a biographical play. Only one person in the parish spoke more slowly than the elderly Irish priest—me. I was cast to play John Coleman as a seminarian in Ireland. The real Father Coleman sat front row center, flanked by Bishop Topel and Sister Bernadette Mary.

The curtain opens to four seminarians sitting around a book-strewn table. One of them says, "John, what do you think?"

I pause and then slowly say, "I re – mem – ber . . . Ches – ter – ton . . . in his book *Or – tho – dox – y.*"

Sister told me the Bishop bent over in hysterical laughter, slapping his thighs. She added, "His Excellency complimented me on my good casting."

Father Lemieux nudged the Bishop. "Will you two straighten up? We have a ceremony here."

I thanked the Jesuit brothers who constructed our new building. The self-effacing crew didn't know how to respond to the long ovation. Father Lemieux paid warm tribute to the companies, the families and the individuals who financed the project. Bishop Topel sprinkled holy water into pool water.

Resolutions and Revolutions

Father Vincent O'Keefe was right about Father Pedro Arrupe when he called him a "re-founder of the Society in light of Vatican II." Father General Arrupe promptly convened the 32nd General Congregation of Jesuits. Its express purpose was to absorb Pope John's open spirit by reassessing the Society's mission, its operations and its priorities.

Although Pope John was dead by then, his successor, the anti-contraceptive Paul VI had not yet begun wrapping a prophylactic over the Second Vatican Council.

The initiatives of the Jesuit General Congregation took root on the Provincial level in a series of local and plenary meetings and papers. They were called "resolutions". The Oregon Province hired the management consulting firm Arthur D. Little to, well, manage and consult us.

Dave Rothrock, Terry McLaughlin and I made up half of the delegation from the Mount. The plenary sessions at Seattle University were orderly, democratic and exhilarating. Jesuits of all ages and positions mingled as equals. The Arthur D. Little guys photocopied and distributed the resolutions and helped choose the panelists running the meetings.

While we were in Seattle, Father General Pedro Arrupe was coming through SeaTac Airport. Father Lemieux arranged for twelve of us to meet him in a conference room. Arby explained to him why we were in town. The humble, smiling Father Arrupe made a point of meeting each one of us and learning our names. I said to him, "Thank you for giving us the opportunity to remake the contemporary Society of Jesus. In gratitude, we will be only too happy to retain you on as Father General."

He laughed and thanked me, and then he moved on to shake Dave Rothrock's hand.

That Christmas Jerry wrote me from theology school in Los Gatos, south of San Francisco. The note was on a card portraying Maurice Utrillo's *Le Lapin Agile sous la neige*.

> *Sorry the Mt didn't get any resolutions accepted. Some of them I thought were too abstract or idealistic. I honestly believe there is no point having a province conference on the meaning of the priesthood. No one knows the meaning of the priesthood. The only meaning there is to the priesthood (or faith) is the one you expressed perfectly in your 4 pp. letter a couple of times ago: some weird deep intuitive rightness (amid all the wrongness) you find flowing in you occasionally. That's the only meaning there is.*

Meanwhile, a Wisconsin Province Jesuit priest was putting together a network of young Jesuit writers and editors, one from each of the ten American Provinces. Father Lemieux deftly responded to Father William Cleary's query that he was volunteering not one but two men. "You need one from Canada. And both of them have delightful

English names. John Barrett-Hamilton and Paul Swift."

With that, my friend from Winnipeg and I became members of the Jesuit Writers Service. I added a third bulletin board to my Jesuit career. Near the Beadle's daily notices, I posted a description of how the Jesuit Writers Service can help you get published. I tacked up copies of query letters to magazines like *Daedalus* and the Modern Language Association's *PMLA*.

Father Cleary kicked off his Jesuit Writers Service by bringing us all to New York City between semesters. John B-H had a soft, handsome smile. It never left his face once he learned that we were leaving Spokane to fly to New York. We were given rooms at Fordham University and we were given tours of the offices of *America* magazine and a leading Catholic book publisher, who invited us for cocktails at his Connecticut home. John B-H and I traded smiles. We became acquainted with our fellow neophyte editors and writers. I saw some of their bylines for years later. John and I returned on Air Canada. We stopped in a sub-zero Winnipeg. Mr. and Mrs. Barrett-Hamilton graciously served us rye in crystal rocks glasses.

It wasn't as if I didn't already have a full load. I was taking four courses each semester in philosophy and comparative literature. I was also Beadle, a delegate to the Provincial reassessment conferences, a member of the Provincial's Advisory Committee and the editor and marketer of scholarly manuscripts. One of the accepted "resolutions" opened one seat of the Mount St. Michael's Board of Directors to a scholastic. As Beadle, that fell to me. I also volunteered two Saturdays a month at Morning Star Boys Ranch for troubled teenage boys. It was founded and run by my Boy Scout Master, Joe Weitensteiner, who had subsequently become a priest.

I moderated the Sodality of the Blessed Virgin Mary at Holy Names Academy. During a Christmas reception at Gonzaga University, I introduced my Holy Names contact to my mother, who had gone there two generations earlier. The nun proceeded to introduce us to her older companion and tell her what a fine young Jesuit I was. The older nun responded, "You can't tell me anything about Porky Swift that I don't already know. He's a rascal and I'd keep a close eye on him." She was Sister Bernadette Mary, my eighth grade teacher and casting director.

"Please, Sister, you taught me to respect the cloth."

Two Heads Are Better Than One

Michael "Beaver" Czerny was the smartest guy in our class at Mount St. Michael's and Gonzaga University. Like me, he added to his Philosophy major another one in Literature. Unlike me, he brought both breadth and depth to our seminars comparing translations of Baudelaire's poems. He was fluent in French and German, as well as Czech.

Michael's fellow Canadian John Barrett-Hamilton and I scored our first Jesuit Writers Service hit by placing an article of Beaver's in a scholarly journal. John's editorial skills stemmed from his intolerance of bull and puffery. John said his own father edited their family name down from Hamilton-Barrett-Hamilton. And Michael first taught me that "obtain" can be an intransitive verb.

Michael and I had entered the final semester of our undergraduate careers with straight A's in Literature and (except for my B in Ethics) the same in Philosophy. A madman Jesuit dashed any hopes we had for an A in our final philosophy course. In our first class, Father Strangelove announced that the Western World's only A student in Philosophy was Aristotle. He created examinations that consisted of what might now be called "sound bites." He distilled the complex and nuanced ideas of dozens of thinkers over thousands of years onto one sheet of paper. The two sides were blanketed with single-spaced multi-choice questions, true-false ones and fill-in-the-two-inch-blank ones. There was also a two-inch blank in the upper right for the examinee's last name.

At Mount St. Michael's, some of us studied together after dinner in smoke-filled rooms. (Pope John's fresh air campaign also opened the window to Jesuit scholastics being allowed to smoke.) We peppered one another with the philosophical questions of the week. After one of those meetings, Beaver turned to me, "Porky, Father Strangelove demands drastic measures."

"Homicide?"

"No, but you're close." Michael proposed a psychologically revolutionary experiment. We trade places. We trade persons. We trade exams.

In our one-on-one sessions, we often became exasperated with the other one, because he was I. We had to master a philosophical point enough to explain it to our alter ego.

"You dolt!"

"Watch what you call yourself."

For the final exam, the large GU classroom was as crowded as one of Father Strangelove's exam sheets. The co-conspirators picked up each other's exam and then separated. Michael printed **SWIFT** in the upper right, and I printed **CZERNY**.

I occasionally looked over to see how fast Beaver was felling my ontological, metaphysical, epistemological, empirical and aesthetic trees. He never took his eyes off the test. My mind wandered. I would have received an A in Ethics if the professor had stopped muddying the lucid prose of Aristotle's *Ethics*.

The bell rang and we turned in our exams. Outside, we put our arms around each other. We had been conjoined twins, then separated and now hugging. "Beaver, you just taught me the full meaning of *trust*." The results were posted a few days later. Michael earned me a 98. I scraped up a 97 for him. We both got A's for the course. Aristotle nodded.

———————

Those were heady days for me and for the whole country. Recreational and hallucinogenic drugs were sweeping across America. San Francisco reveled in the Summer of Love. From nearby, Jerry continued his "Merry Christmas!" note to me.

> *George Kramer is leaving from here to get married. Bernie Lyons is just leaving. Me, I'm happy. Please, Lord, don't let the roof fall in. The Rector here is very worried about us all—and the faculty.*

In the spirit of the times, Alma College, where Jerry was studying theology, relocated to Berkeley and became a member of the multi-denominational Graduate Theological Union. Jerry and his friends hung around the humanistic psychologist Carl Rogers. They frequented the nascent Esalen Institute in Big Sur. The "human potential movement" was no stranger to LSD and weed.

The Vietnam War rapidly escalated, as did the protests against it. *"Hey, hey, LBJ / How many kids did you kill today?"* In 1968, the anti-war Democratic Senator Eugene McCarthy ran against his own President. After McCarthy's strong finish in the New Hampshire primary, President Johnson announced he was not running for reelection.

In the spring of 1968, the Nobel Peace Prize Laureate Martin Luther King Jr. was still trying to stamp out local fires ignited by racist practices and laws. In early April, Dr. King went to Memphis to support its black sanitary municipal employees. They were treated and compensated much differently from whites doing the same work, to put it mildly.

This American Demosthenes stayed at a modest motel near downtown Memphis. In the early evening before the rally, he exited his second-floor room to talk with his colleagues on the balcony. Shots rang out. In an instant Dr. King was dead. Violent riots flared up in cities across the country. The police and the National Guard responded with even more violence.

The ambitious Robert F. Kennedy tried wresting the anti-war banner from Senator McCarthy in the Democratic primaries. Hundreds of us stood in a dusty parking lot at Spokane Community College to hear Senator Kennedy rail against the war. This was one stop in a western swing on his way to the California primary.

Barely a month later, four of us were painting a room in my mother's home. She wanted to spiff up the place for Jerry's imminent Ordination. Leon suddenly turned up the TV volume. We couldn't believe our ears. Senator Kennedy was shot and killed in a Los Angeles hotel kitchen, after celebrating his Primary victory.

Violence became the new currency of the United States, backed by the government. The body count in Vietnam reverberated back home. Napalm the gooks, tear-gas the spooks and corral the anti-war kooks. America was on fire, literally, politically and emotionally.

Father Schlatter told me to write a letter explaining why I wanted to attend Graduate School at Boston College for a Master's in English. This was news to me. "Father, I didn't know you liked my refinishing of that side table that much? What a reward!"

"Paul, you are not going to Boston College as a woodworker. You are going there to study English literature. We think you have solid credentials in reading, writing and criticism."

"Don't put me on. It was the way I presented the Impressionists on your bulletin board."

"I will have to say, I appreciated it that you did not find room for Renoir."

Many letters went to and from the Provincial Dean of Studies in Portland. The Boston College Graduate Admissions Office accepted me and awarded me a Residential Assistant Scholarship. That meant I would live in a dorm with a pack of thirsty and horny freshmen. Graduate school also meant I wouldn't have to teach high school that year, as would my classmates. I profusely thanked Father Schlatter.

The Roof Falls In

During those weeks in the spring of 1968, Jerry's prayer, "Please, Lord, don't let the roof fall in," fell on deaf ears. On the eve of his ordination, after thirteen years of studying for the priesthood, the Jesuits expelled him. Our mother was beside herself in grief and confusion. Jerry's classmates (and soul mates) were enraged. Father Bill Hausmann, a friend of Jerry's who broke the news to me at the Mount, was almost in tears. I was numb.

The reasons for his sudden and ill-timed dismissal changed like the fog over San Francisco. If they had anything to do with experimenting with drugs and maybe sex, Jerry certainly wasn't the only one who might've aroused suspicion in those flower-strewn days in the Bay Area. I figure it was his *attitude*, not in the narrow sense but the bigger vision. Jerry mentally examined and physically absorbed every nook and cranny of human existence.

One afternoon I brought a soft shoulder to my mother to cry on. In the house we grew up in, I found Jerry sleeping in my old bedroom. He had just hitchhiked from Berkeley with the $250 the Jesuits gave him. Here was my smarter and wiser and older brother lying in his skivvies on a floor mattress, with nowhere to go.

"I heard the Ordination is off."

"Porky, you have a way with words."

After his dismissal, Jerry holed up in a Berkeley apartment and wrote a fourteen-page, single-spaced letter in four days. He initially intended it only for the recipients of his Ordination invitations, but it was photocopied and forwarded countless times in Jesuit communities across the country.

Jerry's letter became widely talked about because, like a symphony, his prose wove together social, philosophical and religious movements on a scale almost as large as the Second Vatican Council. His literary and emotional baton summoned Wilhelm Reich, Michael Harrington, Bernard Lonergan, SJ, Ludwig Wittgenstein, Jesus of Nazareth, Arnold Schopenhauer, César Chávez and any number of other intellectual, activist and religious visionaries.

4

Even the Boston Cop
Had Read *Ulysses*

My Jesuit Superiors treated me like a grieving widower. They gave me free rein to get to Boston. I shipped off a small trunk of all my worldly possessions (including my Roman collar, which I rarely wore). I said a tearful goodbye to my long-suffering mother. Kathleen O'Reilly Swift was a proud mother of two Jesuits. All those years, though, she often asked us if we weren't taking all of this religious stuff a little too seriously.

I flew to San Francisco to see Jerry and old friends. Jim and Nonny, whom I knew from Paris, were going back to the land. They prepared a dinner of wild rice and bean sprouts. I visited my mother's sister, Ethel, a traditional Catholic who attended Mass at Old St. Mary's. She asked me questions about Jerry's abrupt dismissal. I suggested she ask him. Jerry was looking for his first job since selling women's shoes at The Crescent department store as a teenager.

From the Bay Area, I took a train bound for Boston. The cocktail car was a carpeted lounge with domed windows and cushioned booths, which were all empty. Four steps down, a small bar faced two tables. I fell in with two well-coiffed women in their late 60s. They had just discovered that each of them had played the theater pipe organ for vaudeville shows and silent movies. The sun went down behind us as we climbed up into the dark Sierra Nevada Mountains.

A pretty woman about my age entered the car. The ladies motioned her to join us. Susan ordered a glass of wine. Not long after she received it, a loud crash jolted us. It came from the far end of the raised lounge. The bartender told us to stay put while he investigated. A boulder had tumbled down a mountain and through one of our dome windows. It shattered glass all over that end of the car. One of the ladies said, "I always sit close to the bartender. It sure paid off this time!"

Her new friend added, "But what a way to go! Zonked on the head by a mountain boulder." I couldn't help but think of Jerry's sudden reversal of fortune, how it crashed into our lives like that boulder had into our railroad car. The ladies retired to their sleeping berths. They said they had enough excitement for one evening. The bartender announced last call, so I ordered Susan and me a glass of wine each.

After the bar closed, we went up into the lounge to inspect the boulder in the aisle. Shards of glass surrounded it and it was now on its way to Chicago. Mountain air whipped through the broken window. Susan and I settled in a booth nearer the bar. She was returning to Northern Colorado from the Bay Area, where she had been visiting her parents with her five-year-old son. He was asleep in their berth.

"What's his name?"

"Paul."

"That's a nice name."

"It was my choice, against my husband's wishes. What's yours?"

"Paul"

She laughed. "I knew from the beginning that I liked you." She moved closer and asked me what I did.

"I just graduated from college, and I'm in my fifth year of studying to be a priest."

She took a deep breath and then a sip of wine. "I don't believe you."

I pulled out my Gonzaga laminated student ID card. It pictured my smiling face perched on top of a Roman collar. That titillated her even more than my name. She kissed me. I didn't resist. In fact, I put my arm around her and kissed her in return. I'd had women come on to my Roman collar before, as if it were a challenge to their sexuality. But Susan seemed to be scratching a housewife's seven-year-itch. I was so horny that I thanked the Lord (!) her son was taking up the berth.

The next day, she disembarked in Denver. On the platform, Susan introduced her two beloved Pauls to each other. She wrote down my Boston College address. We kissed goodbye. I received about three letters a week from her all summer. I didn't write back, but I certainly thought a lot about my married, lonely friend.

———————

Terry McLaughlin, who was a year ahead of me in the Jesuits, picked me up at South Street Station in downtown Boston. The Oregon Province had carved out a slot in BC's Graduate English program. Terry had just completed a year, and I was replacing him. He introduced me to Jesuits he had befriended. Father O'Malley, a Classicist who had heard many stories about "Porky," called me "His Porcine Eminence."

For Terry, Boston was old home week. Two of his father's brothers lived in the South End. These proud Sons of Hibernia pronounced the family name *McLocklin* and they welcomed the West Coast Terry into their homes and large families like a prodigal son returning to the Sod.

Terry liked all things Irish and historic about Boston. He reveled in showing me the tourist sites along the redlined Freedom Trail. We dipped into Irish working stiffs' bars that offered beer and a plate of beans and franks for next to nothing.

A student of literature couldn't ask for a better place than Boston and Cambridge. I explored the bookstores around Harvard Square. The whole city, with its more than twenty colleges and universities, has a literary aura about it. Once, for example, I was sprawled on the lawn in Boston Common reading *Ulysses* for a course on James Joyce. A ruddy Irish cop approached me and waved his nightstick that I was not permitted to lie on the lawn. He then asked me what I was reading. I told him. He pointed to my Modern Library hardcover copy and said, "That looks like a pretty fancy edition. Does it include Judge Woolsey's decision?"

This man knew what he was talking about. In 1933, US District Court judge John M. Woolsey, who had read *Ulysses* at least three times, rendered the opinion that the novel was not pornographic, therefore not obscene, and therefore free to be sold and mailed in the United States. The Boston cop described the decision with so much fervor that he started to sit down beside me.

"Hey," he suddenly said. "You're not supposed to be on this lawn." I wanted to invite him to my Joyce class at BC.

New Friends, New Horizons

Many of those attending classes and institutes that summer at Boston College were Jesuits and Roman Catholic nuns. Both groups mingled in the fresh air of the Second Vatican Council. The sisters, of course, had long ago discarded their black habits. Not so for some of the ancient priests I encountered in the Gothic Jesuit residence where I took my meals. (My room was in a dormitory vacated for the summer by undergraduates.) These clerical relics wore ankle-length wool cassocks fronted with forty buttons. Others wore old wool suits, even in the summer. They lived in an era that predated not only the Second Vatican Council but also the First (1869–70).

My fellow scholastics and a scattering of younger priests gravitated to the same table every day. Among them was Father Robert Drinan, Dean of the Law School. He eagerly sought out our thoughts on a variety of subjects—including the Vietnam War, which he adamantly opposed. When he heard my name and that I was from the Oregon Province, Father Drinan asked if I were related to Jerry Swift.

"He's my brother."

"You should be proud of that."

From the way the Law School Dean talked about Jerry's now-legendary letter, I gathered that he had read it with the concentration he'd give a legal brief. If there had been any appeals process in Jerry's dismissal from the Jesuits, Father Drinan would have been the perfect advocate. We became fast friends, eating lunch or dinner together several times a week.

We neck-tied scholastics occasionally ate with the elderly Roman-collared priests. Some of them were friendly and interesting to talk with. A number of them, however, were so Boston-centric that they thought the world ended where the Mass Pike did. They had ventured that far from Boston only because the New England Province Novitiate, Shadowbrook, stood on a Berkshire hilltop.

Twenty years later, Terry Shea, a close friend of Jerry's since high school and still a Jesuit, related a Boston College story that was still making the rounds. At lunch one day in the Gothic refectory, an old Bostonian told me he heard I was from the Oregon Province. He was incredulous. "What on earth is out there? What do you *do* out there?"

I responded, "Have you ever screwed an Indian squaw?"

In the dormitory where I stayed that summer, I began what would become a lifelong friendship with A. J. Antoon. He had just graduated from BC as a New England Province Jesuit scholastic. He convinced his Superiors (with a skill I would see repeated) to let him direct a summer drama workshop for undergraduates. He staged modest plays outdoors all across the campus. They were based on Paul Sills' "Story Theater."

I introduced A. J. to Terry McLaughlin, he who had strutted across the Mount St. Michael's stage as Prince Hal (to Tony Gasperino's Falstaff). Terry was inspired by the Lawrence Olivier-John Gielgud school of Shakespearean performance. A. J., on the other hand, got his rocks off staging productions that recreated the rollicking outdoor Globe Theater of Elizabethan London.

Armed with his Master's Degree in English from Boston College, Terry spent the next two years teaching senior English and directing plays at Bellarmine Preparatory School in Tacoma. He staged Arthur Miller's "All My Sons" before colleges began to.

Meanwhile, A. J. wrote many zany letters of protest and promise. The Yale School of Drama rejected his application. A. J. rejected its rejection in a letter that read something like "Do you realize the mistake you are making?" He threatened to write the Dean himself, the autocratic Robert Brustein. In

August, barely a month before the new academic year, A. J. did just that.

One afternoon, A. J. pounded on my dorm door. "Porky, I need a car—*now!*" As a graduate student from another Province, I had privileges that A. J. didn't have. Two big ones were that I could eat in the Jesuit residence, rather than in the student dining hall, and that I could check out a car any time I wanted.

In the summer of '68, young people were still discussing "The Graduate." The movie brought anti-establishment rebellion to the suburbs. A. J. heard that its director, Mike Nichols, was directing a summer stock play in the Boston area. A. J. wrote him to ask if he could study his techniques.

A. J. didn't hear back from Nichols until that afternoon he told me he needed a car. Nichols called him and asked that he pick him up at Logan Airport. The two became friends. I think that A. J. learned more from Mike Nichols in action than he probably did at the Yale School of Drama, which accepted him that fall.

Six or seven Oregon Province scholastics of Jerry's vintage were attending a BC summer institute on Pierre Teilhard de Chardin, a Jesuit philosopher, paleontologist and geologist. He was also a visionary, whose almost mystical writings invited controversy from Rome. (Note how often controversy accompanies Jesuit writers and activists.). They were studying Theology at Willowdale, a little outside of Toronto. They immediately transferred their admiration and affection for Jerry to me. I bummed around a lot with Bob Jones, who was as down-to-earth as his name.

More than one Saturday night, Bob and I raised mugs of beer in a loud country music bar incongruously located in the heart of downtown Boston. For that matter, the whole neighborhood was Incongruity City. Sad prostitutes strolled and loitered in front of the irrepressibly upbeat and wholesome Your Father's Moustache sing-along bar. The city's legitimate theater district was only three blocks away.

If Bob and I stayed out too late to get the MTA to its Boston College terminus, we had to walk eight long blocks up Commonwealth Avenue. Cardinal Cushing's palatial, grandly fenced and gated estate dominated the neighborhood. He lived and ruled like a Medici or Borgia. He embodied obliviousness to the spirit of the Second Vatican Council, the opposite of Spokane's modest Bishop Topel.

We celebrated Mass in a large lounge in a new dormitory. We young scholastics and sincere sisters liked to think we were the future of the Church, rather than Cardinal Cushing and the equally autocratic Archbishops of Chicago, Los Angeles, Seattle, among other cities with old-line Catholic populations. However, the pronouncements seeping out of Pope Paul VI's Vatican made Bob and me feel increasingly like we were whistling past the graveyard.

Jim Riley was more intellectual but no less fun than Bob Jones. I had heard that my brother, Roger Guettinger and Don Johnson were the smartest in their class at Alma, California. That honor fell to Jim Riley alone at Willowdale, Ontario. Bob and I took him downtown to hear "Orange Blossom Special" over and over, over beers.

Jim said he was working on a project with Dan Berrigan, SJ. "You might be interested in joining us," he told me. Berrigan was the Catholic chaplain at Cornell University. He was also a leading national voice in the anti-war movement, a movement I was becoming more and more attracted to.

Violence ruled the race riots. Stridency fueled the anti-war protests. Dan Berrigan was neither violent nor strident. To the turmoil, he brought the grace of a poet, the perspicuity of a priest and the rascally wit of a son of Irish Catholics.

Jim said that he and Dan had recruited six Cornell wannabe activists to lead community discussions on institutional racism. The project would take place in August in a working-class neighborhood in Yonkers, just north of the City. I told Jim to count me in.

Michael Czerny, SJ

Michael called me from his parents' home near Montreal. He was biding his time before checking into (no surprise) the University of Chicago's prestigious PhD program in the History of Ideas. He said he was coming to Boston College for what turned out to be an extended visit.

Memories of Beaver and Porky pleasantly intruded upon a summer when I was shuffling between the Middle English I was trying to learn and the Joycean English I was trying to comprehend. As a visiting scholastic at BC, Michael Czerny took meals in the Jesuit refectory. I introduced him around. The Law School Dean Drinan was impressed that Michael was going to study at Chicago. They talked about the philosopher Paul Ricoeur.

After A. J. and I introduced Michael to Mary Jane Flagler, he was seen less often in the Jesuit refectory. Mary Jane became distracted from her seminars by A. J.'s whimsical productions in the open air. Mary Jane was a granddaughter of Henry Flagler. He made his fortune at General Motors and then spent a lot of it as the pioneer developer of the St.

Augustine area. Mary Jane countenanced little of the high life, except to mock some of wealth's trappings.

She took me on a field trip. Just off Newbury Street, Bonwit Teller occupies a regal building surrounded by lawn and shrubbery. Inside the rarified salons, the sales ladies welcomed "Miss Flagler." Even though I had slacks on, the ladies looked at me as if I were wearing bib overalls and a straw hat. Mary Jane introduced me as her "friend from the state of Washington" as an attempt to explain my lack of refinement.

Mary Jane and Michael rapidly became soul mates. She was engaged to an acclaimed harpsichordist, but she didn't seem enthused. (Do the wealthy still have arranged marriages?) She and Michael talked for hours, over coffee or tea in the student union or strolling through the leafy campus. Their brainy attraction to each other made me think of Pierre and Marie Curie, or Abélard and Héloïse.

A few weeks later Mary Jane Flagler and Anthony Newman were married, coincidentally on Jesuit vow day, September 8.

Years later, Michael's PhD from the University of Chicago was less an academic document than an origami of the Bird of Paradise. Christians call that bird the Holy Spirit, often rendered as a dove. A medieval painter would place that dove above Michael's head. After his ordination to the priesthood, Michael ran the Jesuit Centre for Social Faith and Justice in Toronto for years. From there, his Provincial sent him to the University of Central America in El Salvador to replace the Rector who had just been murdered in a massacre that also took the lives of five of his Jesuit colleagues, their housekeeper and her daughter. Michael played a calm, moral role in the negotiated settlement that finally ended Salvador's twelve-year civil war.

Social justice for Michael was personal. For example, in 1988, during the dawn of the AIDS epidemic, Michael was spending a sabbatical at *l'Arche* in France. Jean Vanier had founded *l'Arche* in 1964 as a network of communities caring for and living and working among people with intellectual disabilities. (David Rothrock spent the bulk of his thirty-five years as a Jesuit working at *l'Arche* and founding a *l'Arche* community in Tacoma.)

Vanier referred a young woman to Michael. Her 28-year-old brother had just died of AIDS and his lover told her that he wanted a Catholic funeral. His parents wanted nothing to do with him; they hadn't even visited him when he was sick and dying. Neither did the Church. She had asked a priest to say the Mass. He balked and made excuses that the young man was not in his parish. Michael arranged and performed a Catholic burial ceremony. Years later he wrote that his first brush with AIDS taught him that a priest's role is not to focus on death but to care for those infected with the HIV virus and to console the victims' family and friends.

From El Salvador, Michael was called to Rome, where he served as director of the Social Justice Secretariat in the Jesuits' Curia for eleven years. Then he went back to "the field." He worked as founding coordinator of the African Jesuit AIDS Network, based in Nairobi and encompassing all of sub-Saharan Africa. That led to a close working relationship with African Cardinal Peter Turkson, who became the President of the Pontifical Council for Justice and Peace in 2009. Michael soon followed him to Rome, where he serves on the Council's Secretariat and as the cardinal's Chief of Staff. When his fellow Jesuit, Pope Francis, released his first solo encyclical, *Laudato Si',* in June 2015, it had Michael's fingerprints all over it, since Cardinal Turkson was a principal drafter of the document.

5

The Antiwar Movement's Jesuit Front

"Swift, are you in there?" Father Bill Bichsel knocked on my dorm door one night. Bill was a Jesuit priest from Spokane, twelve years older than I. We knew each other by name but had never met. He was studying at Boston University and helping out at a diocesan parish in exchange for room and board. Bix, who was totally against the Vietnam War, got in a very heated argument with the old-school parish priest. The pastor promptly ejected him from the premises. "Never come back, except to get your belongings! You are a disgrace to the Roman collar."

"That's why I'm here," Bix smiled. "I need a bed." I pointed to the extra one. Then I walked to my desk, pulled out a fifth of bourbon, uncorked it, and threw the cap out the window. "I think I've come to the right place."

Bill quickly found a new post as an adjunct parish priest. Boston was still teeming with antiwar protests and shenanigans. A chapel across the street from Boston Garden became a "sanctuary," a holy place where conscientious objectors were safe from Federal jackboots. Hundreds of supporters gathered outside. Whatever Catholic parish Father Bichsel served, his big heart was with the congregation inside that church.

One Saturday, Bill told me to meet him at 8:00 p.m., when he'd be done hearing confessions. Then we'd go out. I arrived at the church about ten minutes before eight. A few elderly ladies were saying prayers that Father Bichsel had given them for penance. I couldn't imagine what peccadilloes they had confessed ("I ate one more bon-bon than I should have.") When the last woman exited the confessional, I slipped in. "Bless me, Father, for I have sinned," I said quietly.

"My last confession was one month ago." Then I lowered my voice and hesitantly admitted. "I have committed adultery."

"Yes, my son. Could you speak up a little? Was this adultery with a single or a married woman?"

"Neither," I mumbled.

"With another male?"

"No, Father." I stuttered, "It was with a . . . a pi . . . it was with a pig."

Bix threw open his door and thrust back my curtain. "Thank God it's you, Swift!"

"What if it wasn't me?"

"I've met a lot of fucking pigs at the war rallies, but never a pig fucker."

Thus it came to pass that Father Bill Bichsel attended his first anti-Vietnam-War rally with a porcine fornicator. It was the biggest demonstration yet for Boston. I still tease Boston Red Sox fans that the largest crowd ever to fill Fenway Park was the 1968 celebration against the War. We filled every seat and every aisle, and the field was thicker than any namby-pamby rain tarp. It was thick with peace-loving protesters. The mound, so to speak, featured a veritable Antiwar Hall of Fame. Dr. Benjamin Spock, Pete Seeger. B.B. King, Eric Fromm, Senator Eugene McCarthy. We were losing the war on the War, but we were having a good time doing it.

Bix never left that scene. He spent the rest of his life protesting war and nuclear weapons. His base was St. Leo's Parish in Tacoma (where I never confessed any real or imagined sins with real or imagined farm animals), but his calling took him to high-profile places where the military was up to no good. Bix and his cohorts breached security at the School of the Americas in Fort Benning, Georgia. They intended to pour blood and pray over documents—à la Dan Berrigan. Bix's arrest led to one year in Federal prison. After that, he protested at the nuclear power plant in Oak Ridge, Tennessee. He and his group also broke into the Puget Sound Naval Base in Bangor that housed the largest stockpile of nuclear weapons in our country. His smiling but iconoclastic attitude landed him at least once in solitary confinement. What's that to a man of prayer?

Not one to be blinded by a possible nuclear holocaust, Father Bichsel also served as a pastor at St. Leo's. He created a program of transitional housing and food for the homeless in the tradition of Dorothy Day and the Catholic Worker Movement. Simple and communal. Bix received many awards and accolades, but he only reluctantly accepted them.

Canada Calls, Twice

When the summer sessions ended, the Lebanese-American A. J. Antoon, the Irish-American J. Terry McLaughlin, and I drove Michael Czerny to his Czechoslovakian-Canadian parents' home in Pointe Claire, Quebec, near Montreal. Egon and Winnie, as they insisted we call them, had created a home with garden paths that led millions of miles away from the war and violent racism they had escaped in Czechoslovakia.

Egon designed chandeliers and collected rocks and shells. He spent early mornings tending a delightful disarray of flowers, herbs and vegetables. Michael's father and mine had a lot in common. Neither professed a religion. My dad reasoned, "I don't need an intermediary between me and God." Both married strong Roman Catholic women. Egon Czerny and Paul Swift were born and raised eight thousand miles apart, but their personal, independent philosophies grew out of the same soil.

In the story of the young married couple's escape from the Nazi-controlled Czechoslovakia, Winnie was the culprit. She was a Catholic with Jewish blood. After settling in a small town outside of Montreal, on the St. Lawrence, she and Egon raised two sons, Michael and Robert. Winnie became a prolific potter, sculptor and weaver.

One morning, after a breakfast of cheese, crusty bread, fresh fruit and bowls of rich coffee, Winnie said she had a job for me in the city. Egon, Michael, Terry and A. J. stopped talking about Kurt Weil, Lotte Lenya and Bertold Brecht long enough to bid me farewell. "See you fellows. I'm off to Montreal with Mother Courage."

Winnie's old Mercedes two-door sedan was a workhorse. Egon had removed the front passenger seat to make loading and unloading easier. Behind the driver's seat, we stacked games and toys and little bags of trinkets that Winnie had probably made herself. We set out to distribute them in a children's hospital in Montreal. It was fun sitting in the backseat with the gifts, while the pretty Winnie whisked us along a highway to the center of Montreal. She pointed out a few landmarks, but I was in no mood for tourism. Montreal had recently hosted a World's Fair to celebrate Canada's Centennial, but to me the city was my friend Michael's hometown. In the hospital, I don't know who wore the broadest smiles, Winnie or the young recipients of her good will.

In the Czerny atelier, Winnie sculpted me. I posed for less than an hour. A. J. and Terry teased me. "She's just practicing on you with clay," A. J. said. "Then she'll do me in marble."

––––––––––––––––––

So much for the culturally soothing waters of Canada. Back in Boston, hard-hat war hawks were clashing with hippie doves in the Common. The Jesuits provided the national media with two sharply opposite voices. Dan Lyon, SJ, spewed hawkish articles. Dan Berrigan, SJ, led a group of nine who set draft files on fire in a Baltimore suburb. Francis Cardinal Spellman, the Archbishop of New York, fell in lockstep with John Wayne and Bob Hope in cheering on our troops in Vietnam.

Jim Riley suggested we go to the Democratic National Convention at the end of August in Chicago, Mayor Richard J. Daley's personal police state. In the meantime, he and I hung around Yonkers. The Cornell students I met were juggling many causes. They advocated this and they protested that. In thoughtful discussions, which Jim Riley led, I learned the difference between institutional racism and individual bigotry. As hard as it is to convert a racist redneck to a tolerant person, it's even more difficult to extricate *traditions of racism* built into institutions. Like those municipal workers in Memphis, whom Rev. Martin Luther King Jr. died for.

I became close friends with two young women—Sarah Wunsch from affluent Westport, Connecticut, and Elaine Robbins from working-class Maplewood, New Jersey. In support of starving Biafrans, we three walked in a candle light vigil under the sycamores of Dag Hammarskjöld Plaza, across from the United Nations. We then distributed pleading fliers at a 42nd Street entrance to Grand Central Terminal.

Jim took Sarah, Elaine and me down to the Grand Union supermarket in Greenwich Village. We joined a group of mainly NYU students boycotting grapes. Jim introduced us to César Chávez's right-hand woman in *La Causa*. She in turn introduced us to the featured speaker, the anti-war Senator George McGovern of South Dakota. His audience couldn't have been more than thirty—about the same number that voted for him when he ran for President four years later. Even though the Vietnam War still raged, President Nixon beat Senator McGovern in the biggest electoral trounce in US history.

On our way to the Democratic National Convention in Chicago, Jim and I stopped in Toronto. It was a propitious stop. Jim had been living there for two years studying theology. His friends included two married couples, who lived outside of Toronto in Etobicoke. Tony, Jane, Rich and Annie were in their mid-thirties, good looking, well dressed and blessed with very precocious young children. They were educated and conscientious Catholics. They wisely adopted Jim Riley as their personal envoy to the Second Vatican Council.

During backyard cookouts, Jim and I learned that the four of them were soon leaving on a canoeing expedition on the lakes northeast of Toronto. The next thing Jim and I knew, we were heading to the cool woods of Ontario rather than the hot streets of Chicago.

Tony had reserved two twelve-foot canoes at a marina and general store a hundred miles from nowhere. "Calamity Jane" and "Polk Salad Annie" had packed sleeping bags and blankets for Jim and me. I contributed a bottle each of Kentucky bourbon and Canadian rye. The lakes were placid and the canoeing was easy, even for a neophyte like myself. We made camp each night in a sandy cove. Jim and I gathered firewood, Tony and Rich built fires, and Annie and Jane cooked steak, vegetables and baked potatoes.

Exertion, beef, bourbon and rye animated the campfire conversations. Urged by our curious quartet, Jim talked about Paul Tillich, the German-born Lutheran theologian. He lectured for years at Union Theological Seminary, Harvard and Chicago. He fused existentialism and Christianity. Through ontology, he fused philosophy and theology. What is being? God is being. Tillich's conservative critics, less nuanced in the ways of ontology, called him a pantheist. Sitting around a lakeside campfire in the silent, star-lit woods of Canada made it difficult not to be an existential Christian pantheist.

Inspired by the impending autumn, I recited some lines by Gerard Manley Hopkins. "Margaret, are you grieving / Over Goldengrove unleaving?" Rich asked us what we thought of Pope Paul VI. Jim and I rolled our eyes. "Let me put it this way," I said. "After Pope John's Goldengrove, the Church is now unleaving."

———————

Our idyllic getaway ended with a jolt. In Toronto, we learned that the Democratic National Convention in Chicago had exploded. Fifty-five years earlier in England, say, Jim and I would have been two guys who got so taken with the Lake District that we missed the maiden voyage of the Titanic.

The violent disaster was later termed a "police riot." Under the banner of Law and Order, Mayor Daley unleashed *thirty-five thousand* police and National Guardsmen against only *ten thousand* protesters. CBS correspondent Dan Rather was roughed up inside the convention hall. The mace was so thick that the naked Vice President Hubert Humphrey (a sight I'd rather not see) coughed in his shower at the Hilton Hotel. Days later, the notorious speechifier accepted the nomination as the Democratic candidate for the Presidency. That rubbed the proverbial salt into the very real wounds of the supporters of the prominent antiwar candidates, Senators Eugene McCarthy and George McGovern. During Humphrey's ensuing campaign against Richard Nixon, the campaign button I wore on my lapel said, "What Election?"

Jim was staying in Toronto for more studies. He'd let me know about Dan Berrigan's impending trial in Baltimore for pouring napalm on draft records and lighting them. On the train from Toronto to Montreal, I had a couple of beers in a New Orleans-style bar car rollicking with Dixieland music. Michael Czerny met me at the train station. He was only days away from going to the University of Chicago. "I hope the smoke has cleared by then." Michael brushed aside my comment the same way he did cigarette ashes on his typewriter.

Michael's mother had finished and fired her bust of me. I look better in clay than in the flesh. Winnie wrote me later that I was displayed in a gallery window in downtown Montreal. One afternoon, a class of blind teenagers toured the gallery. Each of them felt the sculptures carefully, some abstract, others representational. One girl touched my bust over and over. She traced my full head of curly hair and stroked my prominent nose. She asked for my name. When she heard "Paul," she went into existential teenage rapture. The girl's other main crush was Paul McCartney.

I hitchhiked from Montreal to Boston. Winnie drove me across the St. Lawrence and deposited me at a highway heading south. She'd soon be driving Michael to an airplane bound for Chicago. She gave her boys unconditional love and discipline. I scrunched out of the back of her Mercedes with my shoulder bag. When Winnie patted and then gripped my forearm, I felt like I was one of her sons.

The highway became two-lane roads and then country lanes. Most of the car rides were only ten or twenty miles. The talkative drivers took me from one village or town to the next. I was roaming the roads of France again, speaking French. I had not been this alone all summer. *Un Monsieur* dropped me off at the border. I started to walk through the empty, two-lane customs station. A guard yelled at me, "You don't just WALK into the United States of America! Come over here!" He asked me for identification. I pulled out my driver's license.

"Oregon!" he exclaimed. "Young man, you're a long way from home." He handed my license back to me. "Welcome to America." I asked him if I was late for the Democratic National Convention.

My First Parish

The autumnal Boston College campus wasn't the same without my summertime friends. I lost A. J., Michael, Bob and Jim for squirrels scurrying across the shaded lawns of Chestnut Hill residences. Expensive brick homes lined the streets. I easily imagined Tony, Jane, Rich and Annie living in this neighborhood. During the many hours I spent as a Jesuit taking long walks and jogging on rural roads, I often pictured myself living in one of the wood-frame houses on the small farms I passed. My commitment to the religious life often teetered on imagining a different life to live. On another side of the BC campus, pine and oak trees shaded a small stone Anglican church. I daydreamed about serving its parishioners and living in the modest rectory *with a wife.* I'll have to say, I've never met the opposite of me, a husband who wished he'd become a priest. Or have I?

My 1968 parish consisted of sixteen college freshmen living on the first floor of a brick building surrounded by lawn. I was their Residential Assistant. My rectory was a large room with a single bed, two easy chairs and a private bath. From a visit to the Huntington Art Museum on Columbus Circle, when Jim Riley and I were doing our Yonkers thing, I brought back a large reproduction of Picasso's "Guernica." I hung it on the wall as my own anti-war statement. I eagerly shared it with my boys. As college freshmen, they had the curiosity of sixteen cats.

Samuel Johnson, William Blake and John Milton, along with other English writers and turgid critics, dominated my studies. While waiting in a slow line to sign up for one of those courses, Jerry Thompson and I got talking. We had things in common. He had just come back from a small-budget tour of Europe. We swapped stories. Like me, he intended to teach high school English. Unlike me, he was married. Jerry and Judy regularly welcomed me to their Brookline apartment to share a jug of wine around an old oak table. And tell stories. Jerry admired the Jesuits, and I admired Judy.

Two wacky Dutch Jesuits were only too glad to befriend someone who had traveled to Boston from as far away as they had, three thousand miles. Pieter was in his eighth year in the Jesuits. Dirk was an ordained priest. They were very liberal, both politically and religiously. Dirk gave me a hardcover copy of the recently published *Dutch Catechism.* Enthusiasts of the Second Vatican Counsel revered it. Traditionalists reviled it. The book was intentionally "undogmatic." Nevertheless, its liberal pronouncements invited controversy. For example, it stated that birth control is a matter of conscience.

Practicing it, or not, should be decided by a married couple in consultation with their pastor and their physician. A Burlington, Vermont, bishop withdrew his *imprimatur* from the American edition. Los Angeles Cardinal McIntyre banned it from church-run bookstores in his diocese. Nuns in Boston refused to display it in their stores. Unsurprisingly, the new catechism's lead author was a Jesuit, Piet Schoonenberg, SJ.

Another Jesuit priest, Dan Berrigan, SJ, was also making controversial news. He and eight co-conspirators, by then known as the Catonsville Nine, were due to stand trial in Federal Court in Baltimore. They had protested the Vietnam War by breaking into a Selective Service office in the Baltimore suburb of Catonsville. They dumped hundreds of draft files into big wastebaskets, and then took them outside. They poured homemade napalm over the files and lit them. As obedient civil disobeyers, they prayed while they waited for the police to arrive. It was all very symbolic.

In October, Jim Riley, the newly ordained Richard Ellis, SJ, and I went to Baltimore for the trial of the Catonsville Nine. Dick drove. He was as smart as most Jesuits, affable and athletic, but he had a few frayed brain synapses. For example, he was studying Theology in Hartford rather than Berkeley, Toronto or Chicago, much less Rome.

A patrolman pulled us over on the New Jersey Turnpike. The portly trooper grimaced when Dick handed him a rent-a-car contract instead of a registration card.

"This might be a problem. Let me see your driver's license." Dick's carried a picture of him wearing a Roman collar.

"Jesus," the Irish cop said. "Er, excuse my language, Father. This is not my day. I pull over a priest in a rental car. Whadda I do?"

The trooper gave Dick's documents back to him. "Father, I don't mean to give advice to a priest. But in the future, try not to exceed the speed limit while you're passing a highway patrol car."

Add *guileless* to a description of Dick Ellis, like the Apostle Nathaniel. Incidentally, he was the only one Jesus chose directly. The other eleven came recommended or introduced to Jesus, including a pack of fishermen from Galilee. Jesus looked at the quiet Nathaniel under an olive tree and proclaimed his newest recruit "a man without guile."

The Trial of the Catonsville Nine

The Jesuit fathers and brothers at Loyola College, in downtown Baltimore, graciously received the three of us. It didn't matter why we were in town. What mattered was that we were fellow Jesuits. My room's screen door opened to an indoor hallway, not out to a back porch. That was my introduction to the South. Given the religious demographics of the Confederacy, of the twenty-eight Jesuit colleges and universities in the United States, only three are in the South. The historically Catholic states of Louisiana and Maryland each have a Loyola College. The Deep South boasts one, Spring Hill College in Alabama.

Every evening in front of the Federal Courthouse, hundreds of people gathered with candles and tapers and hope. My Cornell friend Sarah Wunsch and I were walking to one of them when we bumped into the featured speaker, Father Dan Berrigan. The young Jewish woman introduced me to her radical Catholic chaplain.

"Paul, I've heard a lot about you. And your brother, from Jim Riley."

"Got a match?"

"Jim said you were funny."

"Thanks to your program in Yonkers, Sarah and I have become friends."

"She's a good woman. You two will get along well."

Dan was right. Sarah and I became lifelong friends. Dan and I were close for about four years. One day over the telephone he responded to a proposal of mine with a total lack of political nuance. I was no longer a Jesuit and was working for John D. Rockefeller 3rd on programs of corporate responsibility and social change. I called Dan about a prison reform project. He was involved in that after his own stint behind bars. Dan unequivocally (and wrongly) conflated JDR with his brother Governor Nelson Rockefeller, who had just presided over the Attica State Prison massacre. But I suppose, among visionaries, nuance ranks right alongside guile.

Jim, Dick and I found prime seats in the crowded courtroom. I sometimes sat next to Francine du Plessix Gray, the noted staff writer at *The New Yorker*. As a fledgling journalist, I took notes whenever she did. Hers grew into a book she published three years later, the award-winning *Divine Disobedience: Profiles in Catholic Radicalism*. My notes yielded three articles, which ran over the course of the next two months. None of them won an award, but they ran in three cities and two continents.

Central casting sent the flamboyant, eloquent and longhaired William Kunstler to serve as the lead lawyer for the Catonsville Nine. He shared their righteousness. That's the bedrock of civil disobedience, at least in the case of nine nonviolent, anti-war Roman Catholics. The trial lasted four days. All of William Kunstler's divine bolts of rhetorical fire fizzled at the tip of the American judicial system's lightning rods.

The judge reminded the jury that this was a case of breaking and entering a Federal facility, nothing more and nothing less. The defendants destroyed government property. John Hogan testified that certain government files have no right to exist, like the lists of Jews earmarked for Nazi death camps. Selective Service draft files earmark young Americans to kill or be killed in an unjust war in Southeast Asia. "One single life has more value than any amount of property," John Hogan told the court. "I just want to see people *live*."

The defendants brought a calm eloquence to the courtroom. John Hogan, Marjorie Melville and Thomas Melville were former Maryknoll missionaries in Guatemala. They were expelled for "meddling in internal politics." They testified that the "imperialism" displayed by American troops in Vietnam was also bringing US troops, planes and even napalm into Latin America. That was news to me.

George Mische, an Army veteran, had worked for the Alliance for Progress, which negotiated US foreign aid programs with Latin American governments. George testified that he resigned when he discovered that the money was going for nefarious operations.

Mary Moylan, RN, had worked as a nurse midwife in Uganda. She stressed the sacredness of human life that was being denied in the government's excitement over the burning of a few draft files, while US planes continued to drop deadly napalm on people. Tom Lewis was a high school art teacher in Baltimore. He said he wrote numerous letters to Congressmen. He interviewed no less than Secretary of State Dean Rusk and Secretary of Defense Robert McNamara. He arranged discussions with military officials, who said they were just "taking orders." All of Tom's conscientious activity proved futile. So he was driven to take more drastic measures.

David Darst, a Christian Brother who taught high school in St. Louis, testified that the moral apathy and political deafness of our leaders drove him to civil disobedience. David reminded the jury of Jesus Christ's cleansing the temple of money changers. "Jesus could have been tried for assault and battery," he said. "But that is not the point, that is not the point!"

Father Philip Berrigan, SSJ, Dan's brother, was founder of the Catholic Peace Fellowship and a longtime activist in the civil rights movement. His religious congregation, the Society of St. Joseph, was founded specifically to serve the urban black community. He had been jailed often for anti-racism sit-ins. Phil explained that the formation of his anti-war posture began with Pope Paul VI's cry before the United Nations: "War nevermore."

After the prosecution and the defense presented their summations, the jury filed out. Dan stood up and told the judge that the court had dismembered the nine defendants, leaving them without a soul. "This court is just performing a legal autopsy on our cadavers."

The trial's stark contrast between Church and State (joined only by their mutual love of robes and gowns) became blurred when the jury returned. After each defendant's name and charges were read, the foreman intoned a solemn "guilty" twenty-seven times, as if he were in a cloistered choir.

After the trial, Dan Berrigan and I spent a long weekend together in Manhattan. He took me down to Dorothy Day's Catholic Worker community center in the Bowery. He introduced me to the indefatigable, uncompromising Marxist, socialist and pacifist. Dorothy Day had been filling the mouths and souls of Bowery bums for thirty-five years.

She shook both of my hands. "Excuse me, Miss Day," I said. "As a fledgling journalist, I have to ask you a question, an awkward question."

"I respect that." She was a prolific journalist and author herself. In the Twenties, she wrote for *The Masses* and other leftist publications. She co-founded *The Catholic Worker*, which was her feisty play on the Communists' *Daily Worker* title. Its circulation reached 350,000, at one penny a copy. "What is your question?"

"It's not so much a question. Could you please confirm or debunk a rumor? Did you sleep with Karl Marx?"

Dorothy laughed and turned to Dan, "Do I look that old?" She was, in fact, seventy-one and pretty, especially considering she'd been thrown in jail eleven times for nonviolent, anti-war, women's suffrage and pacifist protests. She turned back to me. "I didn't sleep with Thomas Merton either."

"Eleanor Roosevelt?"

She laughed again. Then her thin lips tightened. "That woman wrote me a very nasty letter once, in her own handwriting. In 1941, I had written that her husband's Declaration of War on Japan was wrong-headed. She took umbrage." Dorothy brushed it off and then led Dan to a modest linen-covered table. She introduced him to the winos, and Dan performed a brief Mass and distributed Communion.

The next evening, Dan spoke at an Upper East Side Episcopal church. I was reminded that he was a poet. A poet, a priest and an activist is not a bad combination. I wrote in an article for the Boston College student newspaper:

> *Berrigan told an audience of New York Episcopalians that he feels raising bond for temporary release or remaining free during an*

appeal to a higher court is in a way compromising one's initial decision to stand at odds with a government that is waging a geno-cidal war. If only for his willingness to sit out his prison sentence as a committed Christian, he can-not be dismissed as a wild-worded poet. He is speaking with his life as well as with his poetry.

Well, maybe, and maybe not. Dan eventually and disingenuously went on the lam from the FBI to avoid going to prison. But that's another story.

As a law school dean, Father Bob Drinan probed me about the trial of the Catonsville Nine, over lunch. His curiosity helped me organize my thoughts before writing an article. It ran promi-nently in *The Heights*. It began on page one and ran to about forty column inches. That pleased the anti-war evangelist Bob Drinan. I also published a slightly shorter version in *The Inland Register*, the Spokane Catholic diocese's official newspaper. That marked my own version of anti-war evangelism, since Spokane is a rigidly conservative city.

My friend Dirk volunteered to translate it into Dutch for publication in Amsterdam. In the mail a month later, I received tear sheets from the newspa-per and a Chase Manhattan Bank check for thirty-five dollars. The byline read *Dor Paul Swift*. Pieter and Dirk toasted me in round-bottomed shot glasses, which were designed to prevent anyone from setting them down before drinking all the schnapps within.

6

Christmas 1968

My only local dorm resident, Tom Russell, invited me to have Sunday lunch with his parents at the famous Ken's Steak House in Framingham. Tom was an only child. Mr. And Mrs. Russell wanted to do right by sending him to a Jesuit college and live on campus, rather than at home. Get to know other students and enjoy dorm life. Both parents were well mannered and well dressed. I wore my Roman collar for the occasion.

We sat at a large round table. I had the impression that the Russell family ate at Ken's Steak House regularly. Tom's father, who was blind, knew the menu by heart. He asked his wife what the specials were. She told him and then turned to me. "Tom told us you're working for your Master's in English."

"That's right Ma'am. It should take two semesters and two summers to complete."

"Well, you certainly are a good writer," she said. "Tom brought home that article you wrote for *The Heights*."

"Thank you."

"We can't say that we agree with what the Catonsville Nine did," Mr. Russell said. "But in your article you clearly laid out the defendants' frustration after trying to act within the law."

"I think it took guts for them to do what they did," Tom said. "And they are practicing Catholics."

"Isn't our country in such a mess?" Mrs. Russell said. "This war has torn our country in two. Two fine men, Martin Luther King and our own Bobby Kennedy, were shot down in cold blood. Riots, protests. I can only pray."

Tom's father added, "I'll have the Salisbury steak special."

Instead of leaving the campus over the Thanksgiving weekend, I hunkered down in the library I'd come to treasure. The stone Gothic building and its book stacks and wooden carrels made me feel like a medieval scholar. I had catching up to do after my trip to Baltimore. I must have typed six or eight long papers that semester.

As the Christmas break approached, two Joes appeared at my door, Cincinnati Joe and Buffalo Joe. They asked me if they could have a Christmas party on our floor. "What do you mean by a Christmas party?"

"A keg of beer."

"And mistletoe?"

"Paul, er, Mr. Swift," Buffalo said, "This is an all-boys dorm."

"I guess I overestimated your party skills."

"Maybe not," Cincinnati said. "We've taken up a collection. We have enough money for a half-keg and about ten bucks for snacks and plastic glasses."

"I see all of your research wasn't limited to the library." I thought back on my own freshman year in Milwaukee—home of Pabst, Schlitz and Miller breweries. At this stage of their lives, beer was more important to these boys than girls.

"How about the deposit?"

"That's where you come in," Buffalo Joe said. They politely gave me my assignment: Drive two miles down Commonwealth Avenue to a big liquor store, lay down the deposit fee and procure the keg.

The party rollicked. The guys drank beer and made fun of their professors. I laughed because I knew more than one of them from the Jesuit refectory. At one point, Tom Russell invited me to his room, which was directly across the hall from mine. He handed me a wrapped Christmas present. "My mother knitted this for you." Inside the box was a pea-green V-neck sweater.

"It's beautiful. It's just what I need for a Boston winter, but it looks store-bought."

"Well, she uses this little machine," Tom explained.

Just then, two guys rushed into the room. "Mr. Swift, come quick. It's Bobby O'Shaughnessy." I raced the down the hallway to find Bobby sprawled on the floor, just coming out of an epileptic seizure. The boys had done a good job tending to him. One of them had even put a spoon in his mouth to prevent him from choking on his tongue.

"Good work, Boys!" *Why didn't someone tell me I had an epileptic in my brood?* I thought to myself.

"Is he going to be all right?"

"Well, I'll take him to the emergency room and have him checked out." *Thank God I had drunk only one glass of beer and had checked out the car overnight, so I could return the keg in the morning.* The hospital wasn't far away. Cincinnati Joe held Bobby's head in his lap in the backseat. The ER personnel said he was "fine." In the morning, I called Mrs. O'Shaughnessy to tell her what her son had gone through and to reassure her that Bobby had very caring dorm mates. Then I returned the keg and got my deposit back.

I wrote Christmas cards and letters to new and old friends and young and old relatives. They totaled eighty-five. I guess I wanted to spread my enthusiasm about my life and work at Boston College as wide as possible.

Joyeux Noël

I spent the most delightful Christmas of my life with Michael Czerny and his family in Pointe Claire, down the St. Lawrence from Montreal. "Family" for Egon and Winnie Czerny was all-embracing. We attended dinners and holiday gathering with any number of Czechoslovakians. They were all storytellers. They spoke in whichever language was most appropriate to the telling—Czech, German, French. I could lamely follow the French, but whenever they broke into laughter over a punch line in Czech or German, one of them would lean into me and translate. I was being inducted into a family. I savored the treatment, because after my father left my mother when I was seven years old, family life and holiday celebrations were what the sociologists now call "dysfunctional."

Egon and Winnie's already funky house was decorated for Christmas with peasant exuberance. They showered me with gifts. I was embarrassed. Michael smiled. In Spokane, he had visited my family home a few times, where my divorced Catholic mother lived alone.

They gave me E. L. Gombrich's hardcover tome, *The Story of Art*. It contained a six-inch bookmark with my name rendered in Gothic calligraphy, no doubt Egon's work. I remember these details because I still have the gifts they gave me, including a glazed ceramic coffee cup Winnie had made, and an artful little vase that, to this day, holds loose change on top of my chest of drawers.

All I had to give in return was gratitude. I also made them laugh by mangling idiomatic phrases. Once, Winnie offered me seconds at the dinner table. "*Non, merci. Je suis plein.*" That was my translation of "I'm full," but in French it means "I'm pregnant."

7

Head over Heels

Towards the end of the year, after I had returned from Montreal, I went to the Jesuit residence for dinner. A coadjutor brother at the switchboard near the front entrance motioned me over. "Mr. Swift, you have a phone message. An urgent one." I was to immediately call Jesse Meadors, a neighbor and close friend of Mother's. This can't be good. I skipped dinner and raced to the telephone in my room.

Jesse told me Mom was in critical care in Sacred Heart Hospital after being hit by a car. She was expected to live, but everything else was up for grabs. If you're in an automobile accident, it helps to be in an automobile. Mom wasn't. She was walking in a light rain in the crosswalk, with the green light, when a young driver going in the opposite direction made a left-hand turn and hit her. The car threw her body about fifty feet. She suffered massive head injuries and broken legs.

Jesse, who was about fifteen years younger than Katie, admired her immensely. We three boys felt the same way about Jesse's mother, Marjorie Meadors. She welcomed us into her big house and fed us freshly baked cookies and cakes. I had a dreaded job in her back yard, but it taught me something about life. Mom would hand me a basket and send me to pick raspberries. The vines had gone wild, the sun was hot, and for every raspberry there were six thorns that loved to draw blood from my skinny arms. The reward, however, was Mrs. Meadors' raspberry pie.

Jesse assumed her mother's mantle and regularly brought us baked treats. She also assumed Katie's mantle and began having two or three drinks in our kitchen on Saturday afternoons. She also converted to Roman Catholicism. I patted Mom on the back for that one because we didn't have a car. Jesse drove us to Sunday Mass.

These memories calmed my nerves as I flew from Boston to Spokane. Before leaving, I had called two friends to sweep up after me, to tell my professors that I wouldn't be around for the first week after the Christmas break. Jerry Thompson would take care of the two classes we both attended. Marty McDonough, a Jesuit scholastic from New York, assured me that he'd look after my dormitory boys. "They're good on their own," I told him. "I already taught them that freedom and responsibility are two sides of the same coin." Marty rolled his eyes.

My mother did not know who I was. She confused me with her brother Joe. She would say, for instance, "Joe, for a nice hotel, they colored this room like a *hospital*. Where's Porky?" she said to my face. "He'd paint it a bright color." This did not look promising.

My father worked at Sacred Heart as a janitor. He knew many of the nurses, most of the nuns and all of the doctors. Paul visited Katie every day. For all the tumultuous years they spent together and apart, they still deeply loved and cared for each other. In his custodial scrubs, Dad held Mom's limp hand.

The bone doctor said she had received multiple fractures in her legs. She wouldn't need casts, but she would be bedridden for a month. Then she would need help walking, then a walker and then crutches. "We're looking at probably five months."

Dr. Lynch said her brain—her mind—would gradually improve. "She won't be the same as she was before, but I'm very hopeful that she'll gain most of her mental capabilities. She'll need full-time attention for about six months."

I telephoned my two brothers. Steve was driving a freight truck in Seattle and living in a one-room apartment above the Daisy Chain go-go bar. The loud music didn't bother him because I-5 traffic drowned it out. He said he'd drive over the following weekend.

Jerry had just moved to Washington, DC, where he was working for the Equal Opportunity Employment Commission. He told me he couldn't get free for probably five or six months.

Wherever I turned, I looked at "five or six months." Dad, who had just remarried his second wife, Mabel, was in no position to take Mom in. He said that Sacred Heart had a short-term facility next to the hospital. "It's sort of a temporary nursing home."

"Mom hates that term, nursing home, and she made me swear I'd never put her in one."

"I know, but they will be able to put you in touch with home-care nurses. They come by and wash her, fix her lunch, put her to bed, maybe fix a dinner and leave for the night."

"Dad, it looks like I'm here for the long haul."

He laughed and poured me another bourbon and water, "Son, five or six months."

Jerry Thompson sent me a telegram from Boston: "When you return, we will momentarily remake the world with a bottle of Scotch." I laughed out loud.

His telegram also reminded me that the fall semester didn't end for another three weeks.

Most American Jesuits, especially the Irish and Italian ones, hang the love of their mother on a pendulum that swings from sentimentality to the adoration of the Blessed Virgin Mary. Accordingly, my superiors in Portland enthusiastically granted my request to return to Spokane for five months to take care of my mother. Ever practical, they also enrolled me in Gonzaga University's Education Block to get my Washington State Teacher's Certificate, so I could teach in a Jesuit high school the following fall.

Mother gradually and steadily improved both physically and mentally. She recognized Steve when he arrived. She knew Dad and me by then. She improved enough that we moved her to the extended care facility that Dad had mentioned, where she would remain until I returned from Boston. It was adjacent to the hospital, so her doctors and Dad could check in on her regularly.

Her mind would still unpredictably soar and nose-dive, like a balloon riding the wind. Once, when I was with her in her new room, Genevieve Wall walked in. The two of them had played bridge together for many years. Mother's eyes lit up. "Look at all these Get Well cards I'm getting! And visits. But, it irks me that Genevieve hasn't made time to come by." We exchanged smiles. I asked her about her sons. I had graduated from high school with Mike, and Fritz was in the Novitiate with me for about a year.

Most heartening about Mother's recovery was the return of affection and her Irish sense of humor. She was genuinely happy to see her sons. We laughed a lot, but then her eyes would glaze over while her mind retreated to some far-off region. Many clichés came to mind: the porch light's on but nobody's home, not playing with a full deck, one taco short of a picnic. My own mother's stairs no longer went all the way up.

Steve had driven over from Seattle, so we were able to get around the snow-covered town. He drove me over to Bea House, a new residence on the Gonzaga campus for Jesuit scholastics. It was named after a leading Biblical and ecumenical scholar of the Second Vatican Council, Cardinal Augustin Bea. He was a liberal, intelligent German Jesuit.

I knew all of the Bea House residents. I told them of my suddenly changed circumstances and that I'd be joining them for the spring semester. The priest in charge, Father Al Morisette, had taught me French in the Juniorate in Sheridan. He welcomed me in French. I told him that in two weeks I had to fulfill a requirement for a Master's by taking a foreign language exam. Al teased me, "German? I remember you also took German. I'd recommend you test in German."

"*Zut alors!*" was all I could muster.

Steve and I didn't have to drive far to enjoy a beer with friends. Across the boulevard from Sacred Heart Hospital was the time-honored Park Inn tavern. It had three distinct clienteles, a magic formula for any retail establishment. During the day, working stiffs came in for beer and roast beef sandwiches three inches thick. At 3:30, the day shift ended at Sacred Heart. Nurses and guys like my custodial father filled the Park Inn. In the evening, college students took over, looking for dates and another pitcher of beer.

Steve and I spent the early hours of New Year's Eve at the Park Inn, before driving through the falling snow to our boyhood home. Snow obliterated the lines of street, yard, empty lot, side walk, even shrubs. We built a fire in the fireplace and toasted our mother. What the New Year held was anybody's guess.

Kathleen O'Reilly Swift was struggling to regain her identity. At the same time she was at the total mercy of others. Perhaps that's what gave rise to her sudden outbursts of impatience. I wanted to do so much more for her than I possibly could. I told her I would return from Boston in late January and take her home. We planned on hiring a visiting home-care nurse. I'd be at Gonzaga, ready to fill in the blanks. She squeezed my hand and told me to hug her. Steve drove me to the airport.

8

Whatever Happened to Theodosia Burr?

Jerry Thompson made good on his promise of a bottle of Johnnie Walker Red. He and Judy and I sat around their familiar Brighton table and "momentarily remade the world." "Momentarily" was the operative word. While my professors expressed concern for my plight, and that of my mother, they made no compromises in what was expected of me academically. Papers to write, final exams to take.

I crammed for the French exam by sitting up most of the night with a bottle of red wine and a French reader. I slept in to the last moment and then rushed over to the examination room. After the proctor handed me my passage to translate, I took my seat and discovered that the spirit of Father Morisette had placed me in the German classroom. By now, I was ten minutes into the exam period. I rushed across the hall and received the French exam. It was a snap, an essay by Gertrude Stein on Ernest Hemingway. I had studied enough Hemingway to translate some words I knew only from the context.

Time lurched to the semester's conclusion. I crammed for exams and finished my final writing assignments. One of them consisted of answering three questions for the required Research and

Bibliography course. In addition to answering each question, I was supposed to describe how I found the answer (*Encyclopaedia Britannica* was not allowed). My favorite was, "Whatever happened to Theodosia Burr?" Theodosia was the highly educated, polyglot daughter of Aaron Burr. After he fatally shot Alexander Hamilton in a duel, he wrote his daughter in South Carolina to join him in New York, whence they'd sail to England. Theodosia embarked from Charleston but never arrived in New York. Her ghost still inhabits the Carolina barrier islands.

Small going-away parties sprang up. My boys in the dormitory bid me sad farewells. My Dutch friends, Pieter and Dirk, produced a bottle of schnapps and those funny round-bottomed shot glasses. "Dirk, as much as I enjoyed, and appreciate, your placing my Catonsville article in that Amsterdam newspaper, I have to tell you I also enjoyed the cartoon on the other side of my page. It looked like the Editorial Page, no less. A woman has her infant at one breast and milk is spurting out the other. Pieter translated the caption for me: 'Suck, Stupid, don't blow.'"

Over dinner, I promised Bob Drinan that I'd become more active in the anti-war movement, more than merely a journalist. "Paul, don't short sell journalists' impact on our political life." It was a prescient observation. Five years later two *Washington Post* journalists brought down the Nixon regime.

Father Drinan later became a US Congressman. He was perfect to represent the Commonwealth of Massachusetts. He was a lawyer, a Jesuit, a law school dean and a liberal. He served for ten years, until the Second Vatican Council's anti-pope, John Paul II, forced him to resign. John Paul did the same, more sinfully, in Latin America. The Polish pope, like J. Edgar Hoover, saw Communists in every corner and under every rug. He removed hard-working priests in Latin America, because the Liberation Theology they taught undermined the establishment Church's hand-in-glove relation with variously autocratic, despotic and military regimes. Their myopias conflated Socialism with Communism.

9

You *Can* Go Home Again

Through a drive-away agency on Newbury Street, I lined up a big sedan to deliver to Seattle. I had done that once in Europe. I drove someone else's car from Paris to Amsterdam. I had hitchhiked across the United States twice, on my way to and from Europe. I had flown between Seattle and New York more than once. But this was my first drive from one end of I-90 to the other. The timing couldn't have more horrible. Snow paralyzed the country. It stretched from New England to the Dakotas.

Outside of Syracuse around midnight, bright roadblocks announced that the New York Thruway was closed. This was not a good time to be practicing the vow of poverty. All I had to my name was fifty dollars and a Texaco credit card. *Wait*! I knew a Jesuit priest at Lemoyne College in Syracuse. Over the phone, I asked for Father Voekle. "I cannot disturb Father at this time of night."

"Please tell him this is Paul Swift and I just shot and killed a man."

"I will find Father Voekle immediately."

Then a familiar voice: "Swift, you *killed* someone?!"

"No, Bob, I just had to get past the switchboard. I need a place to sleep for the night. They closed the Thruway." He gave me driving directions to

Lemoyne. The next thing I knew I was the target of a nervous stare as Bob led me past the switchboard operator. In a gleaming institutional kitchen, Bob plied me with cold cuts, cheese, rolls and milk. What an organization to be a member of! I can travel almost anywhere and be taken in by unquestioning colleagues.

Bob Voekle introduced me to a few fellow Jesuits over an early breakfast. They wished me well, and Bob made sure I had a couple of fat sandwiches for the road. I wended my way south and then drove west on snowy two-lane highways overcrowded with long-distant semis, because the Interstates were closed.

I saw my first dry highway in South Dakota. Even the stars were out. I stretched my travel legs by going eighty-five miles an hour on an empty highway in the middle of the night. Empty, that is, until a flashing red light came up behind me.

"I clocked you at ten miles over the speed limit."

"Officer, I interpreted the speed limit as any logical person would. Go slower if the road's wet and crowded. Go faster when it's dry and empty." My logic fell on deaf, helmeted ears. He told me to follow him into town. When he turned his patrol car around, I briefly considered gunning mine and heading to the state line. But Murdo was not near any state line.

We arrived at the white-shingled courthouse at the same time the judge did. He got out of his car wearing an overcoat over flannel pajamas. He fumbled for a key to unlock the small building. Inside, behind a desk, he kept his black coat on, parodying a judicial gown. Whenever I spoke, he slammed his gavel down and said, "Contempt of court! Five dollars!" My protests and his gavel brought the ransom to eighty-five dollars. "Your honor, I don't have that kind of money."

"Settled. Two nights in jail." They eventually agreed to let me go after they took the last thirty-five dollars I had. I resumed my trip west.

―――――――――

Katie complained a lot after her brain injury. Wouldn't you? She was still bedded in the building adjacent to Sacred Heart. "Porky, they took my cigarettes away." She had finished smoking one and threw the butt into the bedside trash bag. It caught fire. Mom pressed the buzzer a number of times. After no response from the under-staffed facility, Mom laboriously doused the fire with a glass of water. "I save the day, and they take my smokes away."

The homecare nurse we hired to take care of Mom once we got her home was no Florence Nightingale. She complained that Mom needed help all the time. *Well, yes.* We fired her. Her replacement was marginally better. We learned that the pickings of home healthcare workers were slim. Jesse Meadors and I helped out evenings and weekends. Jesse lived three houses away and I was living in Gonzaga's Bea House three miles away.

I became reacquainted with the strikingly beautiful Elizabeth O'Reilly. She was a senior now. She was drawn to me because she shared my mother's maiden name. Her father and my mother's brother were the only two O'Reilly families listed in a phone book for a city of 240,000. Her full head of wavy dark red hair was the same color as my two older brothers'. We pretended we were cousins, but, alas, not kissing cousins. The previous year, I had invited her to an open house at Mount St. Michael's, one for which I served as Master of Ceremonies. Now I invited her to our home to meet my mother. I cooked a bottom round steak, Tater Tots and broccoli for the three of us.

A month later, Father Neill McGoldrick stopped me as I walked across campus. "Paul, I want to apologize for entertaining bad thoughts about you." Elizabeth O'Reilly worked for him and had mentioned that she had dinner at my house. "I thought you had, well, carnal intentions. Then I learned you were taking care of your sick mother."

"No need to apologize, Father. I wanted the two of them to meet. Each is an O'Reilly. And who isn't attracted to Elizabeth?"

"Maybe a desert hermit," he laughed. "A blind hermit."

"Another reason you don't have to apologize is that you didn't tell anyone about your suspicions of me. You just *thought* them."

"Paul," this gentle priest said, "thoughts can be as harmful as actions." Father Neill had a finely honed sense of morality. He put me to thinking about the Seven Deadly Sins, and which ones were mental and which were physical. Envy and pride eat at the mind. The body hosts gluttony and sloth. Lust and wrath begin in the mind and then take over the body.

"Father, if you had told anyone that you suspected I was having impure intentions towards Elizabeth, my mother would have chastised you with one her favorites of Jesus' pronouncements: 'It's not what goes into the mouth of a man that defiles him. It's what comes out of it.'"

"I'd like to meet your mother," Father McGoldrick said.

"Sure, you can console my battered mother, while Elizabeth and I are in the back bedroom."

"I'd heard you were a funny guy."

"Who says I'm joking?"

10

Crayonology

To get a Washington State Teaching Certificate, a person has to complete the four courses that about twenty of us were yawning through at Gonzaga. The group comprised fellow Jesuit scholastics, seniors and a scattering of people like my old high school pal Jack Delehanty, who had a Master's in Drama and intended to teach high school. The Education Block was a farce. Even the senior undergraduates, mostly young women, considered the courses easy A's. Our professors didn't even have PhDs, they had *EdD*s. We unfairly joked about them. "Was her dissertation on Crayonology?"

The undemanding academic load left us with a lot of time to party. Jack and his wife, who had a roomy apartment near campus, hosted many evenings. Beer and wine lubricated us, but sexual electricity lit the night like lightning. Bolts struck when Jack's oversexed wife hit on one or another of us undersexed Jesuit scholastics. Sheet lightning also appeared, at least for Dick Anstett and me, when we'd get discussing A. S. Neill and his *Summerhill* and Paul Goodman and his *Growing Up Absurd*. These two books—these two revolutionary thinkers—

contradicted most of the pedagogical concepts we were learning at Gonzaga, although *Summerhill* was assigned to us by one of our professors.

My brother Jerry turned me on to Paul Goodman. He became an inspiration to the New Left student movement of the 1960s, although Goodman himself repudiated that movement for what he saw as a New Orthodoxy.

Dick Anstett and I were able to act out the anarchical tendencies that A. S. Neill and Paul Goodman aroused in us. One of our courses relied heavily on playing roles. Each of the eighteen of us took turns being the teacher, leading an entire class in his or her major. The rest of us acted as the students. Dick and I quickly became the class cutups, sitting next to each other in the back row. We rationalized, and the professor agreed, that part of the role-playing was to train and rate the teacher in handling a typical high school class.

Dick and I made a pact that neither of us would disrupt the other one's classroom presentation. His turn in front of the class came before mine. As a history major, he gave a class on the events leading up to the American Revolution. I sat still. He would occasionally eye me warily, but I kept my peace. My fellow "students" subtly turned their heads back towards me. After about ten minutes, Dick asked the class, "What was the reaction of the Colonists to the Stamp Act of 1773?"

This was perfect for what I hadn't even planned. I raised my hand. Dick reluctantly recognized me. "You know the answer, Paul?"

"The B – B – B – B - B," I drew my stutter out long enough that the entire classroom broke into silent laughter. "The B – B – B - Boston." Dick patiently encouraged me to continue.

"T – T – T – T – T - Tea."

"Yes, Paul?" Dick retained his composure.

"P – P – P – P – P —

"Party." Everyone clapped.

What a perfect trio of hard consonants for a stutterer: B, T and P! The professor gave Dick an A for his presentation and commended him for the way he spontaneously handled my stuttering act.

Along with the Spring blossoming of crocuses and lilacs, we budding teachers were let loose for a month on the Spokane School District's high schools as student teachers. I was assigned to Lewis and Clark. My father's mother attended when it was called Central High (subsequently renamed in honor of the Corps of Discovery). My father also attended Lewis and Clark, where he distinguished himself as one of the fastest sprinters in the country. My brother Steve also went to LC, distinguishing himself as his graduating class's biggest party hound. They slapped me on the back that I was now teaching at Lewis and Clark.

I taught two classes daily, freshmen and sophomore English. To this day, I remember the sophomore teacher's name, Mrs. Carswell. President Nixon had just nominated G. Harrold Carswell to the US Supreme Court. Against widespread charges that Carswell had a "mediocre" legal mind and record, US Senator Roman Hruska (R. Neb.) said:

> *Even if he were mediocre, there are a lot of mediocre judges and people and lawyers. They are entitled to a little representation, aren't they, and a little chance.*

It sounded like the Senator had borrowed a speechwriter from Vice President Spiro "If you've seen one ghetto, you've seen them all" Agnew. Carswell was not confirmed. In a twist of history, the eventual nominee, Harry Blackman (approved by the Senate 90-0), went on to write Roe v Wade.

At Lewis and Clark, Mrs. Carswell was anything but mediocre. She was an engaging teacher. I learned that from watching her in action. There were some bored guys, but no one like the play-acting cutups Dick Anstett and me. I taught a class on Robert Frost's poem *Birches*.

> *When I see birches bend to left and right*
> *Across the lines of straighter darker trees,*
> *I like to think some boy's been swinging them.*

It's a wonderful poem full of many levels of meaning, a principal one being "getting away from the earth awhile" and then coming back. Its last line reads: "One could do worse than be a swinger of birches." After the classroom emptied, one boy lingered. By his age, Earl looked as if this was at least his second year as a sophomore. "Mrs. Carswell probably told you. I ain't the brightest kid in class."

"That's why you're in high school, Earl. To become brighter."

"Anyway, until today poetry was just mumble jumble to me. But you—Robert Frost, really—opened my eyes."

"In what way?"

"I'm a swinger of birches. When I'm working on my car engine, I'm getting away from the world for a while."

I smiled at him and said, "One could do worse than be a fixer of engines."

Earl smiled back and clutched his books as if this were the first time he ever held them. Moments like that, teachers have told me since, make their entire careers worthwhile.

A fellow teacher and friend of Mrs. Carswell's approached me one day as I exited my freshman class. "Paul, Betty has good things to say about you."

"I could easily return the compliment."

"I have a large model of the Globe Theatre. You're working on your Master's in English, right? You must know a lot about Shakespeare."

"Well, more than the average high school student."

"A friend of mine who teaches out at Shadle Park wants me to do a walk-through of the Globe for her class. But I cannot get away from here. How about if you do it?"

"That sounds fun. The Globe was the Apollo Theater of Elizabethan London."

"You're on the right track. Except I don't think there are any blacks at Shadle Park. I'll sign you up for a car and driver."

She was right. Lewis and Clark High dated back almost one hundred years. It was the high school located closest to downtown and to Spokane's version of an "inner city"—no projects, just modest wood frame houses and Japanese neighbors. Shadle High, on the other hand, was built in 1957 in the far reaches of northwest Spokane to serve largely white post-war families.

Speaking of which, many of the male teachers at Lewis and Clark probably wished they were teaching at Shadle Park. They were plain vanilla racists and they despised hippies and anti-war protesters. My long sideburns marked me as one of "them." After two or three lunches with the buzz-cut set in the boiler room, I began eating at a diner two blocks away. It was a mom-and-pop place you'd never find anywhere near Shadle Park.

Jerry finally came to town. Mother was beside herself with joy. Jerry's visit topped off the reclamation not only of Mom's mind but also of her family. Katie was becoming Katie again, whole again. Jerry had rented his car, he explained, with a "bank card." Until then, the only widely used credit cards were American Express and Diner's Club. This new animal, issued by banks, was cheaper and was accepted in much more diverse places. Mother said, "Let's see how it works. Let's eat out!"

After a year of not wearing a Roman collar, I put mine on, with a black suit, and attended Gonzaga University's 1969 Graduation Dance at the Davenport Hotel, the fanciest hotel in Spokane. Nongraduates like Jack Delehanty and me were invited by our Ed Block friends. The Shriners were celebrating at the Davenport, too. I ran into one of them, who was a close friend of my father's. Forrest Baker always teased me about the Jesuit thing, what with the Shriners being historically anti-Catholic.

"Forrest, all is forgiven if you let me borrow your fez for ten minutes." He hesitated, but he had consumed a few drinks.

I entered the Gonzaga ballroom wearing a Roman collar and a fez. I asked a pretty new graduate to dance with me and she quickly complied. We were the satiric hit of the evening.

Tom Bunnell would have none of it. A classmate of mine, Tom was a busybody (and he played the pipe organ and liked Broadway musicals, if you know the type). He wrote the Jesuit Provincial that I had "scandalized" many people by dancing drunk with a woman in the Davenport Hotel. The so-called "scandalized" ones thought our act was pretty funny. The previous fall, Tom and I co-authored an article on Minor Orders, and this was the thanks I received for getting it published in *The Homiletic and Pastoral Review*. Father Provincial sent me a letter of rebuke. In my defense, I wrote back that some people, like dictators and religious fundamentalists, have no sense of humor or tolerance of satire.

11

Puer Pater Hominis

As part of her mental therapy, Mother and I played her beloved game of Scrabble a lot. At one time, she carefully laid down her tiles to spell PIPPLE. "Mom, that's not a word."

"You know, what you lay your head on in bed?" Note the workings of her scrambled mind: she had the first letter correct, the double consonants in the middle and even the same number of letters as PILLOW. Her progress continually showed me the resiliency of the human brain.

Mother's body was healing well, too. As the doctor had predicted, she graduated from bed to walker to crutches. She was becoming independent enough that I was going to leave her for summer school back at Boston College. Her older brother Pat, who called her Kid, came to town. All my life, every couple of years Pat would show up in town with a new car and new wife. He was of the generation that preferred marriage rather than just a shack up. He always brought his kid sister a box of expensive candy and me some toy.

This time he offered us his car. "Take Katie over to Seattle to see Steve." That was music to Mother's ears. She loved to travel, and especially now that she had been cooped up for almost six months. Like most of Pat's new cars, it was new only to him and not to the road.

When Jerry entered the Jesuits in 1955, Uncle Pat drove Mom, her good friend Kath Foster and me to deliver Jerry to the Novitiate in Oregon. It was a vacation riddled with a million laughs. After we'd come into a town at twilight and check into a motel, Pat would excuse himself because he had to "re-charge the battery." After two times, I suggested to Mom and Kath, "Why doesn't Uncle Pat buy a new battery?" They laughed out loud.

Driving Uncle Pat's iffy car on the way to Seattle, I looked over at my mother in the passenger seat. She was very contented, savoring familiar sights as if for the first time. Her hair was growing out after the brain work. She dressed well, complete with nylon panty hose. That spring, I had hoisted her onto a bedpan many times and wiped the location of my human debut. *Puer pater hominis.* "The child is the father of the man."

In Seattle, Steve took us to a favorite bar of his. Mom had a bourbon and water and a small rib eye steak and baked potato. She was forty years old again! We got together with her friend Kath Foster, who was visiting one of her daughters. Mom was becoming herself again, to everyone's relief and joy.

For the return trip to Spokane, I took a side road that wound around Mount Rainier. But before we got that far, Uncle Pat's car died. A small-town gas station mechanic said he'd take it off our hands. Mother and I took to hitchhiking. I stayed back a few feet. I figured a short-haired, middle-aged lady leaning on a crutch waving her thumb on the high-way would do the trick.

She quickly snagged a ride. They were four young people. Mom and I sat in the back seat, with my arm around her. It smelled like the kids had been smoking dope, but I had no choice but to trust the driver. Daylight and my mother went out at the same time. She had weathered a long day and showed her game spirit by hitchhiking. Steve and Uncle Pat loved Mom and the "Kid" all over again when I told them the story. (As far as Pat's car went, he said, "Detroit has more of them.")

Higher up, the mountain was still covered in deep snow, but the roads were clear. The driver negotiated any number curves and cutbacks. He then delivered Mom and me to a gas station on the outskirts of Tacoma. In a pay phone booth late at night, I once again put my fate in the hands of an unsuspecting Jesuit. I called Bellarmine Prep. Rodney Herold answered the phone. "Swift, what a coincidence. I was just going to call you over at Bea House. But now you come to me. We're going to live together this summer in Boston."

While Rod drove Mother and me to a motel, he explained that he was going to study at Boston College. Five Jesuits had rented a house in a run-down black neighborhood, to provide a "pastoral presence" (Vatican II poppycock). I was one of them. "Why didn't anyone tell me?"

"I'm telling you now," Rod the scientist said. "Your letter is probably back at Gonzaga. I just got mine yesterday."

12

Anatomy of Criticism

Rod was right. My summer school stint put me living in Dorchester, next to the notorious Roxbury ghetto. Like the voice-over in Charlie's Angels the priests in Portland directed me to Worcester, where I'd find a car for the commute to BC. Sure enough, in Worcester a Jesuit, who was headed back to the Pacific Northwest, handed me the keys to a '66 Dodge.

The three-story wood-frame house on Woodruff Avenue became a popular gathering spot. The kids loved the new white guys on the block. Eight-year-old Peyton was so proud of his six-year-old sister's voice that he'd summon us all to the living room and tell us to be quiet. With poise and self-confidence beyond her years, Roselle belted out Motown classics with a voice that combined Aretha Franklin's and Ethel Merman's. We applauded her enthusiastically. None of the kids would accept candy or small change. They just wanted to hang out.

The vivacious children were a pleasant relief from my increasingly abstract graduate studies. My focus had evolved from the body of English and American literature to the theory of literature and, even more abstract, the theory of criticism. As an undergraduate, I had taken an excellent course in the Philosophy of Art from Father Louis St. Marie, SJ. In fact, it was almost a tutorial since there were only four of us taking the course that semester. The course hooked me on aesthetics.

My studies veered widely to embrace all that literature embraced. I soaked up Joseph Campbell's *The Hero with a Thousand Faces*, which is a tour de force of the world's mythologies. I studied Mircea Eliade's *The Sacred and the Profane* and *Patterns in Comparative Religion*. Eliade pointed me to the writings of Ananda Coomaraswamy, the Ceylon-born philosopher, metaphysician and art historian. His writings bridged East and West.

As odd as it might sound, in my six years as a Jesuit, I had not taken one course in theology. That hole was now being filled by Joseph Campbell, Mircea Eliade and James Frazer's *The Golden Bough*. Those writers' thinking ranged across the entire world's religions, myths and literature.

That proved a liability when I took my oral exams. Four English professors asked me straightforward questions about prose and poetry, and I'd ramble on about theories and aesthetics. I did give one short answer, though, to their question, "When did Milton go blind?" I replied, "About six months before he wrote *On His Blindness*."

Fortunately, I had one additional tutor who anchored my intellectual perambulations to my final objective, which was a Master's Degree in Literature. Northrop Frye's *Anatomy of Criticism* became my Bible. I studied every chapter and verse and applied Frye's concepts to every paper I wrote. The structural principles of literature "are to be derived from archetypal and anagogic criticism, the only kinds that assume a larger context of literature as a whole."

Frye's analyses complemented the studies in mythology I learned from Campbell, Eliade and Frazer.

> *Natural phenomena yield to mythology structural principles, which are built up from analogy and identity, so the structural principles of mythology—ritual and dream—become in due course the structural principles of literature.*

I wrote a lot that summer, in a sunny upstairs bedroom on a crude typewriter placed on a crude table. This was usually after Rod Herold and I had driven from posh Chestnut Hill to the up-by-the-bootstraps neighborhood surrounding Woodruff Avenue. All my writing wasn't for coursework. The Oregon Province was staging another "reassessment" plenary session at Seattle University in early August. I contributed a long paper to the congress. I purported to speak for disenfranchised young and liberal Jesuit scholastics. The paper rested on the metaphor of "opening the basement door."

After the summer sessions ended, the same Portland powers that had rebuked me in June now flew me across the country to participate in the Province-wide meeting. I was at the university for only four or five days, but the time was exhilarating. I reconnected with guys I had studied and partied with at Mount St. Michael's. My "basement" paper brought me a thumbs-up from many contemporaries, as well as a few progressive priests. One of them, the gregarious and uncompromising Father Justin Seipp, boasted to me that I was *his* for the next year, as if he had reeled in a marlin. This empire builder was the principal at Bellarmine Prep in Tacoma.

Back East, my Cornell friend Sarah Wunsch invited me to her family home for a weekend. It wasn't as if I were her boyfriend; Dennis Groves played that part, clear into marriage. Sarah's home on Campo Parkway in Westport, Connecticut, stood next door to Justice Abe Fortas'. His politically forced resignation from the Supreme Court precipitated President Nixon's nomination of Harrold Carswell and the equally unacceptable Clement Haynsworth, both from the South. Nixon characteristically put narrow political concerns—in this case licking the boots of Dixiecrats—above the good of the nation.

Mr. Wunsch presided over a large Sunday dinner laid out on a table surrounded by his sons and their wives and girlfriends and his daughter and . . .

"I understand you are a Jesuit studying to be a priest."

"Yes."

"So, what are you doing with my daughter?"

"Mr. Wunsch, I think the best religions dance across a spectrum of belief and practice. For example, I understand you are Jewish. But I've never seen a bigger Sunday family ham dinner than this one right here."

"You are indeed a Jesuit," he said. Everyone laughed and Sarah gave me an approving kick under the table.

13

Spiritual Exercises on the Rocks

The Society of Jesus requires its members to make an annual spiritual retreat, usually about a week in length. After Ignatius of Loyola converted his life to Jesus in 1521, he retreated to Montserrat's barren rocks and caves north of Barcelona. He fasted and prayed and began writing *The Spiritual Exercises*. It's a detailed series of meditations, each pointed towards making a *choice* for good, for Jesus, or for bad, for Satan. The retreatant is guided by a spiritual director. *The Spiritual Exercises* has become one of the principal spiritual guidelines of Christianity, not just of Catholicism.

New Jesuit novices, under the direction of the Novice Master, engage in The Exercises at full bore—that is, four full weeks of silence, meditation and writing down one's progress towards sainthood. The demands of the retreat sent a few of my classmates packing their bags, but many of us reveled in the other-worldly experience.

For my retreat in August of 1969, I arranged to have Father Dan Berrigan as my spiritual director. He was back as chaplain at Cornell University. I drove the old Dodge sedan to Ithaca and a rented room where Sarah Wunsch had lived.

Dan lived in a ground floor apartment with a nice back patio. He began the week by saying he once took his retreat at the Trappist abbey in Gethsemani, Kentucky, His director was the famous author, mystic and pacifist Thomas Merton. "Tom took me out to his writer's cabin in the woods. I was quickly reminded that I was in Kentucky. He pulled out a bottle of bourbon.

"So, I want to imitate the Master." With that, Dan produced a bottle of bourbon and two rocks glasses. "Here's to Tom, who died last December."

Dan and I adhered to an easy-going but consistent structure for the week. We met for an hour or so each morning and then again during cocktail hour. In between, I meditated and wrote down *lumina*, the Jesuit term for a spiritual diary. Unsurprisingly, Dan's focus was less on theology than on social conscience and civil disobedience. In fact, one of my meditative texts was Thomas Merton's *Faith and Violence*, subtitled "Christian Teaching and Christian Practice." In it, Merton excoriates wealthy white Christians (and their middle-class clones), who are waging war in Southeast Asia and in the ghettoes in American cities.

Dan was working on a play about the trial of the Catonsville Nine. When I arrived each morning, I found him on the sunny and secluded patio with a huge manuscript on the table. The court reporter in the Federal Courthouse in Baltimore was so impressed with the defendants' testimonies that, on his own, he transcribed the entire four-day proceeding *nine times*. He gave a copy to each defendant. Dan was turning his into a play.

In 1971, as a recently former Jesuit living in New York City, I went to the opening of "The Trial of the Catonsville Nine." The West 50s setting was both a church and a theater.

Here's a short tale of art imitating life imitating art. I was at the original trial, and then I looked over Berrigan's shoulder as the poet distilled millions of words into the ninety minutes of drama I was now watching. The actor portraying William Kunstler stood for his final summation to the jury. Then he quietly stepped aside. From the audience, the *real* William Kunstler took the stage and delivered a shortened version of the speech he had given three years earlier in Baltimore.

14

Criticism of Anatomy

Father Mike Schultheis, an Oregon Jesuit studying at Cornell for the summer, called me on the phone to welcome me to Ithaca, just as I was packing my car to leave. He invited me to a Saturday afternoon faculty cocktail party. As we drove there, Mike asked how my brother Jerry was doing. "He was the smartest, most articulate and most curious mind of our generation. What they did to him was unconscionable."

"Well, Mike, I don't know the bastards' thinking. I've been meditating on the three vows this past week. Poverty's a snap, as long as they give me a nice car like this." Mike laughed. "Chastity is probably the most common reason why guys leave the Order. But the elusive vow of obedience . . . It lies in wait, camouflaged by the benevolence of most of our superiors."

"Well put, Paul."

"Jerry's abrupt dismissal showed me that by taking the vow of obedience, we voluntarily become subjects of a totalitarian regime."

The Cornell party was not short of pretty faculty wives. I gravitated towards five of them in a circle of white wine glasses. One of them was describing her pregnancy. I tried insinuating myself into the conversation. "So, when are you going to have your baby?"

She icily informed me, "I *had* my baby two months ago." Ever since that embarrassing moment, I have never made the slightest reference to weight in the presence of a woman.

Mike wanted to show me the house he was renting for the summer, on the outskirts of Ithaca. I steered the old Dodge through a wonderful landscape of generous lawns, an abundance of shade trees, and deep narrow gorges carved by the advances and retreat of the last Ice Age—the same forces that created the whole Finger Lakes District, long narrow lakes running north and south.

I parked the car on a grassy field across the country lane from Mike's house. Mike and I ascended the wide porch steps and entered the living room. Then he ushered me to the kitchen, where we heard pounding on the glass of the back door. A woman was screaming hysterically, "Your car's on fire! Your car's on fire!" Mike told me to go back out the front door to see what she was screaming about, and he'd try to calm her down.

The woman was right. Flames leaped out of the engine of my car. I told Mike to call the fire department and returned to the front porch. All the books and clothes I had for the summer were in the trunk of the burning car. Just as the volunteer firefighters approached the scene, the car started driving itself across the lawn, headed towards a gorge. It was an electrical fire, which found its way to the ignition switch, lurching the car forward in gear. The firemen didn't know whether to extinguish this car driving itself towards the abyss, or to pray to it.

Mike joined me. "Well, Paul, you're really embracing your vow of poverty with this one. Your car is gone and your earthly possessions are not far behind."

I introduced myself to the firemen, who were dragging out hoses. When the car reached the gorge, a big tree blocked its dive into the chasm. The car's front end wedged against the tree and the back end shot up in the air. The chief said we had to open the gas cap so they could fill the tank with water—-before it blows up. We all looked at one another with trepidation. "It's your car, Pal. Open it." I slowly obeyed, and the chief immediately stuck a water hose inside the gas tank.

A collective sigh of relief swept through the crowd. The fire was out. After I popped open the trunk, the guys helped me retrieve my scorched belongings. I thanked each one of them.

"Say, Mike?"

"Yes?"

"Could you give me a lift home?"

This was not the last of Father Mike Schultheis's encounters with a shabby or burning automobile. For forty years, he worked in poor, war-torn countries in Africa. He built three universities from scratch, often in dire and dangerous circumstances.

Father Dan Berrigan, who had recently been sentenced to Federal prison for setting fire to draft records, delighted in autographing my charred copy of a book of his poetry. We flew to La Guardia on Mohawk (Slohawk to locals) Airlines.

From Manhattan, I took the train to Washington, DC to see Jerry. I got drunk in the bar car, so when I arrived at Union Station I was hell-bent on being Elmer Gantry decrying the sins of the United States Government. It was not a city I wanted to visit. Jerry calmed me down. We had a picnic at Mount Vernon. At dusk, we made a pilgrimage to the Jefferson Memorial. We traded stories from our youth. We sent a postcard to Mom, and I arrived in Spokane only days after it did.

She was in good health and good spirits and living on her own, with frequent visits by friends and neighbors. She talked about selling the house and moving into an apartment—not any old apartment, but one in a new high-rise perched overlooking the Spokane River. It was owned by the Catholic Diocese of Spokane and offered subsidized housing. It was also within walking distance to Our Lady of Lourdes Cathedral, whose adjacent grade school Mom had graduated from. It seemed ideal for her. The only rub was that there was a waiting list; it would take time to sell the house anyway.

Her head injury had left her a little childlike, so I told her I was proud of her research into the new apartment. I also told her I'd get over from Tacoma as often as I could.

15

Bellarmine Preparatory School

After flying across the country three times in one month, then watching my car go up in flames in Ithaca, I opted for riding the Greyhound from Spokane to Tacoma. The change of buses in Seattle made me never want to see that station again. Rod Herold picked me up and drove me to the Bellarmine Prep Jesuit quarters.

If you're thinking that the only thing Rod and I had in common was driving each other around—me at the wheel in Boston and Rod in Tacoma—you're almost correct. Unlike me, Rod was a scientist, a literalist. Unlike Rod, I was a wordsmith. But we shared a virulent hostility to the Vietnam War. Both of us sported the protest movement's signature long sideburns.

The Principal, Justin Seipp, was an intense and driven man. He was about forty years old and was determined to make Bellarmine the best prep school imaginable. He had the administrative skills and pushiness to make it happen. He was creating an excellent faculty. He favored teachers with a Master's degree, like Steve Anstett, the older brother of my friend Dick. Justin also hired one of the first females to teach in an all-boys Jesuit high. His pushiness came in handy during the recruiting bouts for scholastics to teach in the Oregon Province's four high schools.

David Rothrock, who had lived in France (with me) taught French. Terry McLaughlin, with his Master's from Boston College, taught English and directed the drama club. The higher-ups in Portland assigned me to join two of my best friends. I was to teach Sophomore English, Freshman Latin and an Advanced Placement English Lit seminar. I also inherited the award-winning student newspaper, *The Lion*. The Advanced Placement seminar had Justin Seipp's fingerprints all over it: *three* of us, heavily loaded with graduate studies, led only *six* students in a course earning college credits. Terry McLaughlin introduced me to the other seminar leader, Steve Anstett, in his cramped office. "So, Paul, tell me about the Boston Tea Party."

"Of, c – c – course." Steve headed the English department and, at 6'3", was Bellarmine's basketball coach. He was a refreshing departure from the coaches I'd had met so far, including those at Lewis and Clark and now Bellarmine's own football coach. Ed Fallon was a crew-cut war hawk who resented having a woman on the faculty.

My string of excellent rectors and mentors—caring and effective priests like Mike McHugh and Arby Lemieux and Bob Drinan—continued with Bellarmine's Father Tom Williams. He was as laid back as Justin was exuberant. We two slow talkers immediately took to each other. Tom gave me free rein with the newspaper.

Justin was a stickler for discipline, but he also gave free rein once he'd hired you. For example, in my sophomore English class I was reading a lurid passage from Norman Mailer's *Miami and the Siege of Chicago*, his graphic take on the 1968 Republican and Democratic national conventions. While I was slogging my class through the mud and muck and entrails of the Chicago stockyards, Father Seipp opened the door. (Jesuit principals routinely made unannounced classroom visits.) I stopped reading and my boys uniformly turned their heads towards the Principal. Justin motioned me to continue reading, almost apologizing for the interruption. He intently listened to Mailer's raw journalism for five minutes.

Antiwar Marches and Rock Concerts

Crisp fall air, poplar leaves turning to red and the football team scrimmaging up and down a grassy field added up to the best All American autumn I'd enjoyed since I was a high school senior. The year 1969 added two new thrills to the mix: anti-war marches and open-air rock concerts. I met with two women who headed the Tacoma Moratorium Committee Against the War. They enlisted me as their Radar O'Reilly. I typed up and photocopied notices for distribution. The University of Puget Sound was fertile ground, as was Bellarmine Prep itself (notwithstanding grumbles from Coach Fallon). Dianne took fliers to a downtown coffee house where disillusioned Army soldiers from Fort Lewis sulked.

The Lion newspaper deserved every award it had ever received. It was tabloid size and printed on a white matte paper, rather than newsprint. The front page was typically wild and crazy, splashed with photomontages. But the other seven pages lined up in columns of news, opinion and reviews. My two Johns, as I called them, were Editor and Managing Editor—and later the Salutatorian and Valedictorian of their graduating class. They were smart and enthusiastic, leaving me with not much to do— except type articles and keep an eye on an elastic budget. I also ran interference with the printer, which was easy because the students' creative projects were a far cry from printing raffle tickets and church bulletins.

Our first collaboration was a knock-your-socks-off hit. The front cover featured the hottest rock singer in the Northwest, Merrilee Rush. The "Angel of the Morning" loved performing for the kids in Bellarmine's gym. A collage of photos swirled down the page of *The Lion*, not a right angle in sight. Strobe lights, screaming teenagers and close-ups of Bellarmine students jumped off the page even though it was all in black and white. The photographer Paul Brown was a member of our Advanced Placement seminar, as were all of the seniors on *The Lion* masthead.

The Lion became the popular voice of Bellarmine Prep. The debate squad asked for more coverage, as did Father Carmine Sacco for his annual food drive. Paul Brown photographed the bald smiling Italian crouched among towers of canned goods. Rod Herold, who was another exception to the crew cut coaches' lineup, requested a feature on his cross-country running team. We promoted Terry McLaughlin's staging of Arthur Miller's "All My Sons."

The Rector, Tom Williams, congratulated me. "All I did, Father, was tell the printer where to send the bill."

"I passed it along," he smiled.

The two Johns wanted to produce a Homecoming edition. It would be the same size and look as *The Lion*, but only four pages of photographs and captions. "What's the hook?" I asked them.

"The Year of the Banana," they answered. I couldn't argue with them, because I didn't know what they were talking about.

With Paul Brown in tow, they visited faculty members and staff in action. They'd hand a banana to a teacher facing a class. He'd accept it, and Paul got his shot. From behind an administrative desk, the stern Justin Seipp was caught examining a banana. Even Coach Ed Fallon was pictured questioning the banana in his hand. The Coach's appearance was a natural since the newspaper was the main souvenir of the homecoming football game. The cover of the issue featured a blow-up of a banana, running the length of the page. It was another triumph, which simultaneously celebrated football and disarmed the protagonists with a banana.

Meanwhile, I became Co-Chairman of the Tacoma branch of the Moratorium Against the War, along with one Lil Maylott of the University of Puget Sound. Our march was a huge (if pyrrhic) success. Under sunny autumn skies, hundreds of people walked solemnly on neighborhood streets and sidewalks. I saw the parents of some of my students. I wore a Roman collar and carried a white cross. So many students from Bellarmine and the girls' academies marched that they filled the campus chapel afterwards, SRO. I gave a short homily.

The next morning, Rod Herold defended me against the grumblings in the teachers' room. "Aren't we supposed to be teaching our students how to think and form an opinion?"

My next-door neighbor in the Jesuit residence was like Rod. Jerry Weller frequented labs more than libraries. He was a longhaired chemistry instructor with strong opposition to the Vietnam war. I often thought that the most impassioned opponents were scientists, rather than Lit majors. Take Doctor Spock, for one. Albert Einstein, for another.

The Jesuit residence was populated with the usual egalitarian mish-mash of scholastics and priests. We had separate shower stalls, with doors, but you couldn't get away from Father George Dalquist's cigar smoke while he showered. "George," I asked him once while we were toweling off. "How do you keep it lit in a shower while you're soaping up?"

"Paul, I place it across the soap dish after I have removed the bar." I have always admired Jesuit precision.

The Two Johns, two or three reporters and I met for a meeting to map out the next issue. "What do you have in mind for the editorial?" I asked. *The Lion*'s editorial took up a fourth of the page. Students, parents and alums all avidly read it.

That fall of '69, outdoor rock concerts across the country flowed like lava from the Woodstock Festival volcano.

"That dumb-ass Seattle Archbishop said going to a rock concert was a mortal sin." "That flat-ass cross-dresser doesn't even have the *authority* to define a mortal sin." These sons of Catholic schools knew more about moral theology than the Archbishop of Seattle. I told them their editorial was lying on the table. "Just skip the swearing. Use logic. And full sentences."

About three weeks after *The Lion* editorial lambasting the Seattle Archbishop appeared, Tom Williams knocked on my door. "Paul, I hate to bother you, but I'm with a conference table of disturbed parents. They are upset about *The Lion* editorial criticizing the Archbishop. Could you come and appease them?"

"So, Tom," I teased, "You couldn't handle them and now you have to bring in the A-Team."

"Paul, I am not a journalist and you are."

"You mean you read my article in *The Homiletic and Pastoral Review*?" Two of Tom's strong points as an administrator were trust and delegation.

After the introductions, I asked the parents if they'd rather have their sons hanging around the boys' room, complaining and swearing about the Archbishop's autocratic ways. Or have them sit down and use the logic and writing skills that you are paying the Jesuits to teach them. Write an editorial. The Archbishop is welcome to reply in a letter to the editor. (He did and we published it.) An hour later, Tom Williams knocked on my door again, "Paul, you dazzled them. I knew you'd stay away from that First Amendment falderal."

"You mean the Right to Bear Words?"

The entire front page of the December issue of *The Lion* featured a freeform, blank verse Christmas poem by Bill Petrich. We printed it against a muted gray background of the Madonna. Her flowing veil followed the poem's spiraling lines. Bill's literary sophistication belied his age. He had a subtle command of allusion and metaphor and internal rhyme.

Bill was a shooting star. He died in his early 20s. From his obituary, I learned he was the nephew of Father Bill Costello, SJ, his mother's brother. My brother Jerry knew Father Bill at Gonzaga U. He once recited to me a poem of his that praised pruning. Pruning encourages new growth. When I read the young Bill's obit, I hoped that his poetry published in *The Lion* pleased, in some small way, this sister and mother of two poets.

16

The End of My Rope

I spent the Christmas holidays with my mother in the house I grew up in. Friends asked me to parties, which I didn't attend. I even turned down the invitation to a New Year's Eve bash at the home of my high school friend Jack Delehanty. Instead, I tucked my fragile mother into bed for the night. I poured myself her drink of choice, bourbon and water. Then I stoked the fire in the fireplace I'd known my whole life. It was right in this spot, in June 1963, that Mother asked me what I was doing for the next school year. I told her I was entering the Jesuits. Jack, who was sitting on a sycamore trunk next to the fireplace, said, "Katie, you're lighting the wrong end of your cigarette."

I sat on the davenport facing the flames and reflected on the previous months. One picture blurred President Lyndon Johnson and Pope Paul VI. The encyclical *Humanae Vitae* and the Gulf of Tonkin Resolution became the marriage papers of Church and State.

My Jesuit vows were wearing thin. Poverty was no problem, because I was a Socialist at heart. Neither was the vow of obedience, because I served under a string of reasonable, even enlightened, Jesuit superiors. Chastity was a different story. For example, I once took the Rector's car to attend a Bellarmine basketball game halfway to Seattle. At the game, I bumped into Kathy, who was an Irish lass with a boyish figure I'd known from the previous spring semester at Gonzaga. I drove her home. We made love in front of her apartment in the front seat of the Rector's car. I should say she made love to me. At least I wasn't wearing my Roman collar. But, still, the Rector's car? This was not right.

A year earlier at Gonzaga University, a Jesuit scholastic music major with a better sense of rhythm than humor hanged himself to death. He left this note: "I've come to the end of my rope."

In front of the fire in the fireplace, I concluded that I, too, had reached the end of my Jesuit rope. I could not in a clear conscience represent, much less defend, Church teachings I didn't agree with. In the moral sphere, the prohibition of contraception had not only shattered my own parents' marriage, but also that of millions of other sincere couples. Its arbitrary morality was dictated by dogma-obsessed Church Princes. They were recapitulating Thomas Aquinas' sarcastic remark about counting the number of angels who could fit on the head of a pin. *Humanae Vitae* lined up with the earlier Papal pronouncements of the Pope's infallibility and the physical "assumption" of Jesus' mother into heaven. Each was designed to draw the faithful into a tighter, more unquestioning faithfulness.

Closer to home, my grasp of the vow of poverty took a beating when I visited the new Jesuit faculty house at Seattle Prep. These priests, who rank among the better high school teachers in America, deserved their new, well-lit, modern facility. But the television room almost made me puke. Rows of plush chairs faced a giant screen, like in a Hollywood producer's mansion. I can't say it was the moral equivalent of having sex in the front seat of the Rector's sedan, but it came close in my idealistic (and naïve) mind. Then again, poverty dictated that the faculty all share one TV set, rather than each of them having one in his room.

Still, which I was that night in front of the fireplace, the Seattle Prep faculty house was not a Jesuit lifestyle that inspired me. It was one more sign that the Jesuits and I were coming to a parting. But wait a minute! How can I leave what I *am*? It's not like walking out of a room. It's like walking out of my own skin.

Not Alone

I was not alone among the disillusioned religious who were initially attracted to serve the Church in its hopeful days of the late 1950s and early 1960s. A couple of years earlier, I wrote an article for the Gonzaga campus newspaper: "The window that Pope John XXIII opened to let some fresh air into the Church is being used just as often for priests and nuns to jump out of."

The British Charles Davis was a clear-minded and articulate theologian, who sat at the front table of many Second Vatican Council meetings. In 1967, Reverend Charles Davis abruptly left the Church and the priesthood. He wrote a best-selling book about his decision, *A Question of Conscience*. I gave it to my mother for Christmas. It was probably one of the least appreciated gifts ever put under the tree. Her Irish Catholicism was of a simpler sort.

The Kalamazoo Kavanaughs were a remarkable Irish-American Catholic family, with no shortage of brainpower. Four of the seven brothers became medical doctors. Two became ordained priests. The seventh took over the family's insurance business. Son Number Four, Father James Kavanaugh, earned a PhD in Psychology from the Catholic University of America. He also studied the Philosophy of Theology in Germany. Many of his professors bristled at his liberalism. One of them, Joseph

Ratzinger, eventually became Pope Benedict XVI, yet another pontiff in a series of dogmatists who dismantled Pope John's pastoral initiatives.

For all of his academic achievements, Father Kavanaugh preferred the parish life. He served for nine years as a parish priest in Lansing and Flint, Michigan. He counseled married couples. Many of them struggled to be good Catholics, but they confessed to Kavanaugh that they just couldn't afford to have more children. (*Humanae Vitae* strikes again!)

In 1967, under a pseudonym, Father Kavanaugh wrote a piece for *The Saturday Evening Post*'s "Speaking Out" column. "I Am a Priest and I Want to Marry" garnered the heaviest reader response in the one-hundred-year-old magazine's history. The columnist Abigail Van Buren wrote Kavanaugh directly: "I have received hundreds of thousands of letters, but this is the first fan letter I've ever written."

A few months later, Kavanaugh's first book, *A Modern Priest Looks at His Outdated Church*, was published. He excoriated the Church, which he said was bogged down in medieval concepts of sin, hell and guilt. With his schooling in Clinical Psychology and his years of counseling married couples, he set out to confront such sacred taboos as pre-marital sex, contraception, divorce and remarriage, married priests, the works.

Asked why he wrote the book, Father Kavanaugh said, "The Church had done a lot of damage to people's personal lives, and I felt compelled to say so."

A Modern Priest immediately hit *The New York Times* Bestseller List and remained Number One for eight months. The book, and the courage of the author writing it, drew praise from *The New York Times* ("an anguished plea"), the Trappist monk and author Thomas Merton, the Chicago priest and novelist Andrew Greeley, even the Benedictine Cardinal Gregory Baum (another theologian of Vatican II fame), among countless other publications and religious leaders. As I said, I wasn't alone in feeling jilted by the Church I had embraced.

A Damaged Life

Midnight approached. I checked in on my mother. She lay sleeping. Before Mom was hit by a car walking in a crosswalk and thrown onto her head, she was hit and thrown by the Catholic Church. My father wasn't a Catholic and he had no patience for the rhythm method. (Full Disclosure: If my parents practiced birth control, I would not exist. Only after I'd grown up did I realize why Mother called me her Love Baby.) They eventually divorced.

In her 40s and 50s, my mother was a single mother before its time. She was lonely without the man she loved. She led one of the damaged lives that James Kavanaugh said the Church fostered. Mother occasionally dated. She even had a boyfriend for two or three years, who was stationed at Fairchild Air Force Base. But those interludes of happiness must have regularly sent Katie to the Confessional. Not to mention that the Church forbade her to remarry, even after a divorce she vehemently fought.

I kissed my sleeping mother's cheek and wished her the best for the new year. I poured myself another ditch, put a log on the fire, and sat back down on the davenport.

Choices are more than the sum of the reasons leading up to them. There's always something else going on. On my first day in the Novitiate, our new class mingled under scrub pine and oak trees to get acquainted. I asked the Novice Master what were the odds of any one of us taking vows two years later. Father Mueller replied, "The Holy Spirit does not deal in odds."

My choice didn't come only from Seattle Prep's plush television lounge, or from my roll in the Rector's hay wagon, or even from Pope Paul VI's *Humanae Vitae* encyclical. (Consider this: If the Athenians had not sent the Apostle Paul packing his bags for Rome, the Catholic Church might now exhibit Grecian grace rather than Roman law. In the Greek Orthodox Church, for instance, pastors marry, as Father James Kavanaugh proposed. It doesn't seem that complicated.)

I made the soul-soothing decision to leave the Society of Jesus. I had hitchhiked to Jerusalem in search for the historical man from Nazareth. As a Jesuit, I found Jesus living in the hardworking and holy priests I was privileged to know. I raised my glass to Fathers Mike McHugh, Connie Mullen, Fredric Schlatter, Phil Soreghan, Arby Lemieux, Robert Drinan, Bill Bichsel, Dan Berrigan, Mike Schultheis and Tom Williams. I also toasted Dorothy Day and David Rothrock, two of a kind. Then I put another log on the fire.

Paul Swift
Tybee Island, Georgia
September 8, 2015

Afterword

I add this letter of my brother Jerry's at the risk of making my own narrative look like Forrest Gump paired with Stephen Hawking. Jerry wrote this letter in four days following his sudden expulsion from the Society of Jesus, after thirteen years of academic and religious preparation. A week earlier he had been ordained a deacon, which is the last step before ordination to the priesthood.

The only changes I've made to Jerry's letter are to add the title, the subheads and three footnotes, and to make a few minor edits to the text.—PS

A Theology of Creation

Berkeley, California
Friday, May 24, 1968

Dear friend of me or my family,
  especially those I love—you know who you are,

You know that announcement of my ordination as a priest we sent you last week? Well, this letter cancels it: I will not be ordained in Spokane on June 8th. As of Tuesday, May 21st, I am being dismissed from the Jesuits for what Superiors take to be my beliefs and practices regarding sex and psychedelic drugs.

123

Much of what I am charged with is false or misunderstood. But there remains the basic fact (which I have lived with for a long time and which keeps this from being a great shock to me) that my values differ markedly from traditional Jesuit values, and that involved in my complex dedication to the Society, and within the Society, to larger values, has been the daily risk that a radical incompatibility might crystallize between us. [*Yes, that is one sentence. Fair warning: Others like it will follow.*—PS]

As many are doing, I have tried for the sake of religion to accommodate myself to the Society, but without compromising myself. For all of us this is walking the razor's edge, not to be unbendingly authentic on the one hand or shamefully unfaithful to what we are on the other.

From the point of view of my life as a Jesuit, I became a fatality along that razor's edge. It was in the cards always as a possibility, and I faced and lived with that possibility. Taking reasonable risks for the sake of important values is the kind of living I believe in.

From my own point of view, I am not a fatality or failure in any sense. My dismissal is in no way an interruption or breakdown of my dedication to the welfare of men—to what Christians call "the kingdom of God." Rather it is a further development in the on-going history of my dedication. "It is necessary that these things be suffered for the sake of the kingdom of God. The kingdom of God is brought forth only in travail and groaning."

The Society and the institutional Church were not ends but means through which I could be of help in shaping the new creation, the kingdom of fire and music. And as a means to this end, they are far from ideal; so that much of my immediate dedication had been to work for the refashioning of the character, methods, and role of religion in the world, especially by doing what I could to bring the Society and the Church into wider experience and commitment to a turned-on, painful, explosive world. So, it was my concern for the Society that led to my dismissal from it.

History Is No Respecter of Persons

Let me explain in more detail. (If the detail sometimes gets boring, just skim over it.)

The Jesuits, yes you Jesuits, made me who I am. I am thinking now especially of those of you who stand with the traditional Society, who neither sympathize with nor understand the ferment of the 1960s. From my 14th to this my 32nd year, you Jesuits have been my sole and single educational and social matrix. I am the product of your system, of your world. I believe that world with all its pomp is passing away.

Try as you might to multiply yourselves unchanged—as though by mitosis—the process has lately, perversely, turned fertile and it is, with the fixation of a biological drive, producing a new being as though by meiosis, a new man for a new age. Not just me, not just us scholastics, but increasing numbers of students, who disavow your faith, your patriotism, your intellectual presuppositions, your social values, your meaning and what you are.

History is no respecter of persons. In the logic of our common history, what <u>you are</u> leads to what <u>we are</u>. That's no justification of us, but neither can it be any injustice to you. We are both sincere; though we differ, we are intimately related—as effect and cause. I am honestly grateful to you for the way you have formed me; I feel you have prepared me for what is to come.

What disappoints me is that you seem to have lost faith in me, <u>in your own work</u>. If we, the young,

125

are not to ready the Society for the future, who is? Or do you allow yourselves the luxury of assuming the Society does not have to change? Now that I am gone from the Society and can no longer be any sort of threat (if I ever was), please let your judgments go for a few moments. Try to see what elements of truth there are in what we are saying and attempting to do for the sake of the Society, which we love as you do.

Role of Religion in Our Suffering World

For me in particular, as I have said, this personal development within the Society centered about the role of religion in our suffering world. For me religion is the sense that living amounts to more than rational daily experience and is the attempt to live in response to that mystery of being. It is belief in the transcendent in the sense that the meaning of our lives transcends any positivism, any reductionism of life to its simplest or most obvious parts. It transcends any foreclosure of the human longing to understand and be loved.

Organized religion, such as the Catholic Church and the Society of Jesus, takes as its role to facilitate among individual persons and in whole societies the embodiment of this sense in their patterns of living. Mystery becomes flesh. Mystery becomes the flesh it has spun. Meaning incarnated, embodied. Since men and societies differ widely and change constantly, weaving its mystery back into the fiber of the world calls for a unique adaptability on the part of institutionalized religion. It calls for Jesus' remarkable freedom from compromising cultural and political entanglements, his freedom from rigid commitment to philosophic, theological or moral theories, his clear freedom from the inertia of attachment to property, prestige and power.

It is not easy for a massive institutional religion to remain as personal and free as the individual religious man, Jesus, was. But difficulty is no excuse for giving up, as Charles Atlas teaches. It is reason for trying all the harder.

If religion is to serve the *anawim*—the needy—whom Yahweh loves and his prophets serve from Amos and Isaiah and Chavez, institutional religion must with all of its strength resist acculturation to one stratum of society. It must resist cultural identification with the values, fears, interests and insularity of any one class in society, especially of course, the ruling class, the law-and-order class.

In our society that is the middle and upper-middle class. For those of us who know only its world and have all we have because of its well-functioning systems, we are scarcely conscious of a "middle class" and can find little patience for critics who talk of its "evils."

But for the disinherited, the dispossessed, the culturally deprived, for the blacks, for Mexican-Americans, for the white poor, those who live in ghettoes and slums, for intellectuals of dissident beliefs, pacifists, and conscientious objectors, for the chronically sick, the mentally retarded, the physically handicapped, the old, the insane, the unemployed, for miners and migrant farm workers, for Michael Harrington's other America, life is hardly a beautiful dream.

For the dispossessed, there is such a thing as the middle class. From the outside it is a gigantic, cruel, impenetrable system of systems, which in its fat and swelling opulence leaves them too little food to eat, too little air to breathe. The American industrial-military-technological compact, the unconscious but brutally rigid patterns of our social life, the 100-billion-dollar leviathan of federal bureaucracy, our vast public and private educational systems, the brutal realities beneath the glossy surface of our goods-and-services complex, the cellophane and plastic, the immensely rich closed circuit that is organized labor, the endless pap and mush of the entertainment media, our intolerant national ideology, the grim inevitabilities of our insecure and defensive foreign policy—all these middle and upper-middle class systems support and reinforce one another to the exclusion of many Americans.

The system of systems, which nourishes us, is also the *de facto* exclusion of the nation's poor people, of the minority races, of thoughtfulness, and of peace-loving. And exclusion here means hunger, hatred, coercion, intolerance, suppression, injustice, police brutality.

In the face of this exclusion it is clear why the religious tragedy of this century is the acculturation to the middle class of institutionalized religion. That religion should slavishly take its place as just one more devouring dinosaur in the circle of self-containing systems is an abomination of desolation such as even the prophet Daniel didn't dream of.

It is what Carl Amery, writing in his book *Capitulation* about the German church's relation to the Hitler regime, calls *milieu Catholicism*. The essence of the tragedy is that, to the world's hopeless, organized religion has no hope to offer.

It is in many functions the whited sepulcher of the Pharisees, only on a gaggingly larger scale. And not out of bad will, but out of narrowness, insecure self-aggrandizement, the thoughtless assumption of righteousness, the ultimate indifference of the haves for the have-nots, out of cultural under-development, philosophic immaturity, social blindness. This is not to underrate the good it does in ministering to the "religiously inclined" among the middle class. To try to tell you different would be foolish. But Jesus' reaction is clear: *Unprofitable servants!* Another time he said, "The son of man has come not to heal the healthy but the sick."[1]

Admiration of the Society and the Church

I entered the Society 13 years ago in admiration of it and of the Church as they were. Deep within the Society and the Church, I came to know and shudder at their terrible sickness, their terrible failure to love men effectively. Yet never for a moment did I think of leaving. So the dumbfounding truth, as it came home to me year after year, drove me pitilessly toward a much more nuanced and realistic dedication.

Rather than take the Society's and the Church's purpose for granted, I had to do what I could to repudiate their sleepy unreal aim and to shake them both awake. I had to do my best to bring religion into intimate involvement with all men who suffer, whether physically or intellectually, and who live in shadows they do not need to live in.

This evolution, through the years of Jesuit training, in my attitudes toward religion, contemporary life, and their inter-relationships, was naturally long and intricate. There is a subtle chemistry of interaction between the culture and the Jesuits. The individual Jesuit is always the ultimate synthesis of the two. But it is difficult to separate his individual-

---

[1] Francis, the current pope, in a Spring 2015 interview said he would like to be remembered "as a good guy. I hope they say: 'He was a good guy who tried to do good.' I have no other aspirations." He continued, "I became a priest to be with people and I thank God I haven't lost that." Asked why he insists so much on the poor, Francis said that "poverty is the center of the Gospel. Jesus came to preach to the poor. If you take poverty out of the Gospel you can't understand anything because you take out its core."—PS

ity from his collectivities; that is, to separate his continuities with old Jesuit tradition, Western intellectual life, and contemporary American culture from his unique personality and the thrust of his sheer freedom.

The Dialectical Nature of Influence

The Oregon Province likes to think it's all my individuality, and those who know my father see Paul Swift's tough old eye gleaming through mine. I'm maintaining here, on the other hand, that it is self-defeating for the Society to overlook the powerful collectivities I represent. And I'm maintaining that it's simply foolish, as well as self-defeating, to see me as representing only the one collectivity of "worldly" American culture. What I'm trying to say, for the Province's own good in dealing with its young members, its future substance, is that it was the collectivity that is the traditional Society which had the overriding influence on my growth.

If you older Jesuits do not recognize it in me, that is because: (1) you overrate the unchangingness of continuous tradition; (2) you underrate the dialectic nature of influence—historically the thesis rarely yields an identical thesis; more commonly you have an antithesis on your hands; and (3) you underestimate and therefore fail to come to terms with our other continuities, especially our continuity with the current national culture. Implacably that culture is working its chemical will on the Society (in the person, especially, of its younger members, as I have said).

The Society can work its own chemical will on the culture too—and for precisely that did Ignatius Loyola found it. But it cannot do so unless it enters into that culture permanently (adolescent memories and occasional forays are not enough) and becomes thoroughly involved in its chaotic life. The only influence worth the name is God's way of influencing: from within.

Until the Jesuits are trusted by the Society to be wholeheartedly contemporary, the Society will never shed that pale influence she has been struggling to generate since her restoration in 1814. But this will involve the Society's trusting in Jesuits the value and strength of her own training of them. That she cannot do till she understands the subtle chemistry of interaction between culture and the Jesuits. The interpenetration of influence is wholesale (and at present very one-sided, in favor of the American culture); but it may be handy for the Society to consider it under two different aspects.

One is the Apostolate. Here the Society still has to forget her old one-way pride, in the realization that one cannot generally influence without *being influenced*. And that means being influenced beyond the sway of one's own foresight and will. Perhaps it is because it's with the young that there is less danger of *being* influenced that the insular American Jesuits have stuck almost exclusively to education. Jesuits are always saying *Nemo dat quod non habet*, that no one can give what he does not have. But they have yet to realize that this static aphorism must yield to the dynamic principle that *a person who won't receive doesn't have much to give*.

Time's already up for the Jesuits. Their dwindling retreat movement, their unexceptional parishes, their collapsing educational systems, are trying to tell them so. Like many major problems it's so simple at the root. For 400 years Jesuits have thought they had something to give the world. Period. Now history's not giving them much more time to trade in that mistaken assessment. With humility down and regular payments of trust, the correct assessment is theirs: they have nothing much to give the culture unless they elect to receive from that culture.[2] When and if the Society finally internalizes this first law of influence, she will be less eager than she is now to oust Jesuits like me.

Secondly, the interaction between our culture and our Society has important consequences for the training of Jesuits. The Society needs a much sharper realization that she is not training her members all by herself. Once she truly acknowledges the actual interaction of influence as it issues in the mature Jesuit, her system of training can appropriate its own strengths and weaknesses, adapt itself for the first time in decades to the actualities of the case, and ultimately produce Jesuits she can trust. To illustrate this profound interaction, and to illumine the particulars of my own position in the Society at the time of ejection, let me outline briefly that intricate evolution of my attitudes, which I have been speaking of.

The Meaning of Anything Is Its Function

Philosophically I matured out of a static worldview and from an ontology of substance, nature, powers, operation, and immanent natural order, to a metaphysics of emergence and of function. The Jesuit Bernard Lonergan revealed to me that reality is not the already-out-there-now real world that appears to my biologically extroverted eyes. He showed me that the world is ordered and meaningful, not before I know it, but precisely by my knowing it. Reality in the full is not an already

---

[2] A heartening example of this law of influence is Jean Vanier's L'Arche movement. My friend David Rothrock lived and worked in L'Arche, France, and organized a L'Arche community in Tacoma, Washington, where the caregivers and the intellectually challenged live and work alongside one another.—PS

ordered and natured world of independent unchanging essences.

Rather, reality is the achievement of human critical understanding of human experience. Thus the abstract question or bewildered query, *What is love?*, yields to my own efforts to critically understand my own unique love experiences, making each of them what I discover they mean to me and what I want them to be. My world is mine for the making, within the limits of what I discover to be ontologically given and within the limits of my own intelligence, curiosity, creativity, and courage.

Ludwig Wittgenstein taught me that the meaning of anything is its function. The meaning of the priesthood is not simply some intrinsic nature it supposedly has at the nod of the hierarchical church, some substantial character within the permanent structure of God's world. Benz (*Evolution and Christian Hope*, p. 30) indicates how Augustine's positivism concretized the Church in the external authoritative hierarchical church and how, to effectively guarantee the permanent viability of the pragmatic transposition, he institutionalized the priesthood, raising it to the level of a properly characterological sacrament, as eternal and ineradicable in its reconditioning of the individual as Baptism.

The awkwardness and inefficiency of this sort of institutionalizing of the priesthood, especially as we know it now—aligned with compulsory celibacy—is coming clear today, as larger and larger numbers of talented, sensitive, educated men desert the institutional service of the institutional church for the service of people.

The meaning of the priesthood is its function: to heal and to console—and to give hope. The actual priests of God in our time are not discoverable by what oil is on their palms or what honorific titles

133

and letters embellish their names. As Jesus said, they are known by their fruit: a teacher in a minority school, a college professor that lives and says today's truth, the nurse that loves the unloved in a psychiatric ward, the soldier or the seminarian or the assembly-line worker who by what he is touches his brothers' lives with meaning and hope. Priests, whoever they may be, are on duty in the wards of human suffering. As I had said again and again, I wanted to do what I could with my life to make the institutional priesthood an actual priesthood.

The Mystery of God Is Creative Change

Process philosophy (especially Whitehead, Hartshorne, and Wieman) suggested that the mystery of God is not up there nor out there nor even in here in the depths. The mystery of God is creative change, always at work among us. That mystery is not an unrelated Absolute beyond time and change, but precisely the most related and adaptive of all. Right here.

The mystery of God is most influential because it is the most open to influence. (Hartshorne remarks how sad the government of the Catholic Church is, because, most closed of all to being influenced, it is the most clumsy and ineffectual in trying to properly influence.) In those writers and thinkers I saw how the source of human good lies not in any one doctrine or institution or method or idea, but in service to creative change itself, the change that reaches beyond the thrust of its causes, beyond any of our expectations, beyond even our imaginings, simply because it transforms the entire way we look at the world.

The Theology of Guilt and Justification

Theologically, I broke with the theology of guilt and justification: Augustine, Luther, Jansenism, Kierkegaard, Merit Catholicism, and Existentialism.

I broke with the pathological focus on original sin. The doctrines of the depravity of man and the expiatory sufferings of Christ. The no-lasting-city theory of this world.

I broke with Western individualism, the centrality of free deliberate acts, personal responsibility, antecedent and consequent conscience, the vast and minute moral theologies, personal perfection, the private examination of conscience.

I broke with Ignatius Loyola's and Ben Franklin's examen beads, a fault a day, Western personal guilt, rugged individualism.

I broke with private property, the myth of <u>mine alone</u>. The taxpayers' money, the Calvinist ethic, philanthropy, New York loneliness, it's up to you mac, everyman is an island, God 'elps 'em as 'elps 'emselves, the Ockham/Luther/Kierkegaard/Barth chasm between man and God, the Fall, *The Fall*, Existentialist isolation, *The Rebel*, Sartre, Meursault. Add to the separation of man from man, of man from God, the separation of the Redemption from Creation. The Incarnation and Redemption as Plan #2. As for justification, I like Schweitzer: justification is merely the rim on the crater of salvation.

I discovered the responsive meaning and good sense of the theology of Creation and the Spirit: out of Jesus' preaching, the theologies of John and Paul. *Light has come into the world; the darkness isn't grasping it. The world is Christ's. The earth is his body, the fullness of him who fills all in all.* The Greek Fathers. Theology of Light. Of the Spirit. Wind and Fire. Joachim of Flora. Nicholas of Cusa. The City of the Sun. Nikolai Berdyaev. Karl Barth. Teilhard de Chardin. And my own tutor, Fr. Joe Wall. And me. God's creating is the whole of nature and history. (Given evolution, the distinction breaks down anyway.)

The mystery of God breathes the world as an incomplete but emerging process. Its endless ranges of possibilities respond to man's creativity and destructiveness. Evil is not specifically the intrinsic moral character of certain actions. It is the lack of coherence, integrity, and completeness in human existence. Ignorance, selfishness, hunger, mistakes, fear, lack of generosity, loneliness, the misuse of power, sickness, bigotry, cowardice, and whatever else inhibits men from discovering themselves in one another's presence.

God's Ongoing Hope for the Universe

God became human, not to buy back man from Satan nor to do reparation for man's disobedience, but as a basic act in his ongoing creative hope for the universe. The mystery of God became Jesus to give meaning to the terror of human freedom, to the pain of man's incompleteness. The mystery becomes the flesh, which he has made and cast in a complementary dialectic of human longing and creative freedom.

The longing is chaotic. The freedom is chaotic. The meaning of this chaotic dialectic is Christ. Its meaning is the kingdom of God. Its meaning is the body of Christ: chaos pitted against chaos but bound together in one body by the flooding continuity of pain and destiny, sperm and flesh, the spinning orbits of dreams and blood, particles and worlds within a nucleus of hopes bombarded by time is the body of Christ, is love's body.

In the Spirit of God, which dwells in our hearts and is at work and is at play among us, we rationalize the universe that yielded us up. In that spirit we come to terms with our own powers to create and to destroy. We respond to the Spirit of our common bodily existence by acceptance and generosity. By our coming to understand, by our coming to love, the Spirit creates the meaning of the universe in our flesh. And ultimately perhaps in history we men, in the mystery of God's Spirit, will complete the circle of man's freedom and longing.

The morality of the Spirit is not the morality of acts and of law. It is the morality of obedience to creativity, the generosity of loving, and the strength of mutual respect.

Personally, I had not so well appropriated the spirit of the ancient theology of creation, as I had appropriated the insights of contemporary philosophy. But I had been trying, trying to be generous with my gifts, with my affection, with openness about my struggles and breakthroughs. And my uncertainty and weakness; generous too with my strength, my hope, my happiness. I had been learning not to fear—but to risk for the sake of values. I have only one life. If I do not risk it, I will never live it. "If you do not lose your life you will not find it."

Sex

At the same time, I had taken repeated precautions to make sure my risks were reasonable and worthwhile. If anything, I've risked too little, been too indifferent, too clinging to security. I have not had the guts to lay myself on the wind, blowing true, but where I do not know. I believe there are what at least roughly approximate moral constants, though these constants are the object of intellectual discernment, not physical seeing, and though the distinction between acts and their circumstances is a shorthand that cools quickly. Murder, some abortions, nuclear war, stinginess are perhaps examples of such constants.

However, sexual activity, as far as my understanding of human affectivity goes, is not susceptible to any sort of wholesale treatment. I believe no sexual act is immoral of itself. The relevant considerations are the persons involved and these considerations are extremely complex and delicate. But that is no justification for moral shortcuts, such as absolute norms, or the lazy refusal to try to transcend and ultimately dissolve one's hang-ups. In the affective domain I had tried to expand myself, though with care. I have acted with honesty, discretion, and seriousness of purpose. I have done nothing immoral. I don't know what else I can say.

It seems disproportionate to dwell on this matter since I have been so cautious and not overly successful in my attempt to grow affectively. But a society and a Society so hung-up on its own unresolved sexual repressions, obsessions and conflicts is bound, as has happened here, to make a public mountain out of the all-too-modest molehill of my private affective life. That doesn't mean I like the idea of being kicked out of the Jesuits in the name of the sexual immaturity so many of us share.

Well, anyway, the theology of creation is the dying of false guilt, of systematic self-defeat, and of the despairing need to rely only on transcendent hope (hope in the hereafter, in ultimate meaning), which chills men today and seems to mock their suffering. The theology of creation is being born of love of self, overflowing in love of life and brothers everywhere. It is the being born of immanent hope, discovered in our own experience and able to be shared without a word said, a sermon preached.

The Avant-Garde California Culture

Culturally within the Jesuits I grew into concern with what I considered profoundly significant trends of the avant-garde California culture about us at Alma and on the fringe of which Alma is known, has some influence, and is in turn inevitably influenced. We made our first encounter group under Carl Rogers and his staff from WBSI (Western Behavioral Sciences Institute at La Jolla), and the effect on long-range Alma life and Jesuit life in general because of Alma will be immeasurable. My group had Doug Land, perhaps the best of facilitators, and they were all really reassuring to me. That first encounter group experience and the reinforcing of subsequent groups gave me something, which neither professional psychotherapy nor hallucinogenic drugs have done, or could do, I think. Psychotherapy gave me rational insight; psychedelics irrational, subconscious, subterranean insight; and encounter groups the actual experience of my own basic goodness—especially through the repeated gift to me of affection and positive regard.

The three together have been for me an incredibly powerful assault on my immaturity, my childish patterns of self-defeat, my self-hatred and guilt reactions, and my gross underdevelopment in so many areas of my living.

Doug Land remarked after the group that I might make a good group leader, and I later took that suggestion up. That was last spring. Last summer I got into another encounter group in the Stiles Hall program at UC Berkeley (supported by the Danforth Foundation). The facilitator of this group was Gib Robinson, who later became my friend, and is the object of slanderous charges in the Provincial's condemnation of me. Gib generously took me in when the Society dumped me in 13 minutes after 13 years. It is in Gib's Berkeley room and on his typewriter that I am now composing this account of my dismissal.

Last November Gib and I held a very successful encounter weekend for Bay Area educators, during which I led my first group, without distinction. Since then I have led groups at UC Santa Cruz for Esalen Institute. I've had some contact with the Free University movement throughout California, and have been enrolled in the best of them, the Midpeninsula Free U.

Psychedelics

Except for such few and modest contacts, we Jesuit scholastics live rather shyly behind a redwood curtain at Alma. A lovely quiet island about which stream and swirl boiling California currents. The hippie communities in the Haight, in Berkeley, in Lime Kiln Canyon, and beyond Alma at the far end of Bear Creek Road.

Also near us on Bear Creek: New Horizons, where Esalen holds weekend programs; Presentation College, site of encounter weekends; Shantih, the Zen center under Esalen's Gia-Fu Feng. The Sonoma State Seminar in Humanistic Psychology. The Center for Explorations in Education (a UC Davis attempt to coordinate the California Free U's). The New Left, as at San Francisco State and Cal Berkeley. Hell's Angels and the Gypsy Jokers, with whom some of the guys at Alma are involved. *The Berkeley Barb*. Macrobiotic diets and yoga. Rock bands and love-ins. Flowers, beads, transcendental meditation, naked children, sunlight, sharing bread, light shows, oceans, incense.

Sincerely and consciously as a member of the Society and the Church, I tried intelligently to involve myself in the interests of this amazing world. If there is any criticism I would acknowledge, it is that I did far too little. I dabbled instead of really exploring.

Their interest in the body, from Reich to Lowen to Rolf to Gunther to Aerobics to Macrobiotics to Zen to Yoga, I took up as the main intellectual (!) effort of my last year in theology. Christianity is the most important incarnational organized religion, and it has, as of 2000 years after the Word became Flesh, no theology of the human body. That frontier intrigued me.

Their interest in the power and dangers of hallucinogenic drugs I wanted to share. Certainly if contemporary institutional religion ever faced a *coup de grâce* to its effete voice, its unappetizing presence, its bland rituals and colorless "message," to its silently screaming irrelevance, that threat is psychedelics.

Whether in art, literature, music, dress, home decorating, or directly through hallucinogenic drugs—or in the resulting transformation of the individual's sensorium, his heightened awareness, deepened love of color, texture, pattern, of flowers and stars, of small fine things and fresh air, of human flesh and face, his lust for the marvelous body of the ordinary world—in whatever—psychedelics is explicitly and aggressively religious.

If the organized religions have not noticed, it is because psychedelics knows nothing of the sterile Christian eristics and apologetics. Psychedelics knows that the Word became flesh because words don't work and flesh does. So it works its religious magic in flesh, swirls, color clashes, wowing sounds, intricate cool-medium lettering whose sense I must unearth for myself. And to this brilliant plumage of noise and joy, this jungle of color and zoo of sound, the great American religions are deaf and blind, because the only place they've ever thought to find religion is in their own uninteresting hearts, their empty churches, their tired books and sermons, full of words words words full of nothing, nothing at all.

Yes, I got interested in psychedelics. And for religious reasons. I could not help but be hurt by the Provincial's implying that this was a business of off-hour fun, senseless orgies a shade or two more livid than the senseless orgies of low Jesuit expectations allow priests: booze, endless TV, malicious gossip, prodigal waste of time, of unique opportunities, of others' money, and of their own talents.

Ad Deum qui laetificat juventutem meam

Last November, after careful planning and in closely controlled conditions, I took a mild (150 micrograms) dosage of LSD-25. That day alone with myself and a friend was the single most significant experience of my life. To repeat the trite phrase, with perfect accuracy, it was indescribably beautiful and indescribably terrifying. With the help of my experienced guide toward the end of the trip and afterwards, I was able to integrate this incredibly profound experience of myself into the substance of my daily living. I believe it was the greatest single help to maturity I have known.

A psychiatrist who generally repudiates the use of LSD-25 was so impressed with the account of my experiences under it and its subsequent value to my psychic development that he asked me to put it in writing for him to the degree possible.

This spring I considered taking a second trip. I meditated on it for a couple of weeks. I talked it over with friends experienced in hallucinogenics, consulted with the psychiatrist mentioned, and finally decided against the trip for the time being.

Those weeks showed me that what I needed at the time was not more shattering breakthroughs but, instead, a more continuous and profound plowing of the soil of my psycho-nervous system. I needed the dependable knitting, which is conscious integration of more apt patterns of behavior. I do not think my use, or non-use, of LSD-25 has been irresponsible, or incompatible with the kind of man that would make a good priest, as Father Provincial felt. Many other, and much more distinguished Jesuits have taken LSD-25, and much more often and much more publicly than I. I mention only the famous Jesuit theologian, John Courtney Murray.

Cannabis sativa

I have also explored, in my usual cautious and limited way, the blessings and disadvantages of *Cannabis sativa*. At reasonable time intervals and under appropriate conditions, I have both smoked and ingested marijuana. I have also smoked hashish with and without the hookah. My own experience with these mild hallucinogenics has been almost thoroughly enjoyable and thoroughly profitable to me personally and somewhat helpful in my usefulness to others (if we must evaluate things in these utilitarian terms).

Father Provincial suggested that those sexual activities which I am accused of, but which I never engaged in, I committed while unconscious or out of control under the influence of *Cannabis sativa*. As those of you who have experience with cannabis know, Father betrays here a serious misunderstanding of the nature of a marijuana high. All I can do is assert what I know in clear honesty to be true: I have never said a single word or done a single thing under the influence of cannabis that I was not aware of or that I have regretted later. As with many educated people in thousands of cultural pools across the country, the use and enjoyment of marijuana among some communities of Jesuits, both priests and non-priests, is very widespread. I can't argue the case of marijuana here; but I can state as a fact personally experienced over a long period of time: marijuana has most of the

143

advantages of alcoholic beverages and few of the disadvantages, with some important additional advantages besides. Since James L. Goddard, Chief Commissioner of the Federal Drug Administration has said the same in much more thorough fashion, it seems futile to add my voice. But even in futility, facts are facts. This was the charge against me that the Provincial seemed visibly most disturbed at. That it should be a cause for my dismissal from the Society does marijuana more honor than its due. It also does me, and the Society a serious injustice.

In conclusion, my experience with hallucinogenics, even compared to other Jesuits', has been restrained and, if anything, excessively reasonable.

Non-Possessive Love

Lastly, I became interested in experiments in communal living, in new patters of family life (as well as Religious Life), in the possibility of married life without jealously or sexual exclusiveness. But my interest has never gone any further than discussion. A cognate issue is that of clerical celibacy. Compulsory celibacy is unfair to priests and people alike. Successfully human celibacy is a very rare gift. Most of us were not called to that, but rather to Canonical celibacy: no marriage, no overt sexual life. Covert sexual life, involving persons one is not willing to commit oneself to in marriage, is an extremely delicate matter, if individuals are to be carefully respected, if all is to be honesty and genuine interest in the other person, and if any shade of shock or scandal is to be avoided. This is not to say it is impossible. We have yet to begin to explore the possibilities of free non-possessive love.

The experimenting along the lines that I am acquainted with is one of my first reasons for having better hopes for human community, so that, while I have not practiced—as I am accused of—the so-called "Third Way," I understand its context in the social and ecclesiastical developments of the immediate present. I believe it is philosophically and psychologically naïve and theologically recidivist to hold out of hand that it is either good or bad in itself, to say nothing of condemning it wholesale. We are not dealing with a formal world out there of automatic rights and wrongs, which authority can adjust by decree.

We are dealing with individual flesh-and-blood human beings generally more honest, sensitive, educated, responsible, and free than are the authorities who presume to decree.

Besides being influenced in all of this by the diffuse culture about me at Alma, the writings of the later Norman O. Brown, of Marshall McLuhan, Herbert Marcuse and William Burroughs were especially influential in breaking down my own middle-class blindness and numbness to the sharp, lovely, painful world we all really live in, whether we know it or not.

Psychological Integrity

Psychologically, in my personal growth, I, as well as my friends, feel I have achieved a great deal. My psychological integrity is the achievement. The consensus development is nearly 20 years long now. It has been only by way of light years of introspection, lonely reflection, paralyzing emotional struggles all too obvious, hundreds of psychology books read and absorbed, uncounted hours with psychotherapists—to say nothing of the great help encounter groups and psychedelic drugs were to me. This past year I have been so happy (after so many years of struggle and depression) that my superiors required me to get psychiatric certification of my sanity before they would approve me for ordination. (The California Provincial, Father John F. X. Connolly, felt it was an artificial happiness, put on to make sure I got ordained.) I have a sense of psychic integrity now, and I think it is my wholeness and happiness all this year that enables me to undergo such a sudden change of state with easy equanimity and with peace before God, before myself, and before those who love and respect me.

The persons who have helped me in this are too many to mention. Especially important, though, was my friend Gib Robinson, and a psychiatrist, Dr. Julius Heuscher. I suppose as far as reading goes, I have been most influenced by Freud, Theodore Reik, Bernard Lonergan, Karen Horney, Abraham Maslow, Carl Rogers, and Eric Berne.

Reik attuned my third ear, and I became aware of so many more voices in me. Maslow helped me trust them. And he helped free me from the futility of a life of high education and culture spent running away from basic deficiency needs.

Mysteriously, after so many tough years, it was during these months that life began to flow in me more fully, filling in those basic needs. Whetted with hope, I desired for myself Rogers's "personal congruence" of thought and feeling and speech and action. I began to realize the importance, not only of client-centered counseling and student-centered teaching, but of a non-directive emotional life as well. I grew more appreciative of the spontaneous healthiness of my own system. As I freed them and gave them their head, I sensed my drives moving toward convergence. They began knitting into a natural integrity, which gave me my first experience of my own positive identity.

Karen Horney led me to discern my neurotic habits of defeating myself and pitying myself, which is a vicious self-destructive cycle. Eric Berne permanently crippled these patterns of self-defeat and self-pity by ruthlessly exposing their dynamics.

The child in me and the parent in me warring in the presence of a paralyzed adult.

One day I had shied away from a challenge. Gib stunned me with the insightful remark, "Your dad's still winning, huh?" Now, in Berne, I understood. I will not forget Berne's sentence: When you are seriously depressed, your parent is beating the hell out of your child; the only solution is to get your adult in there and separate them. The more I differentiate the dynamics of my emotional life, the more I'm releasing its marvelous many-angled thrust toward organic unity. I sense I am becoming one thing, becoming a person, the person I am.

Civil Rights

Experimental education also drew my attention, educational reform at Alma in particular and a proposed experimental high school for the Oregon Province.[3]

I have done what little I could do to move the Society closer to some sort of de-institutionalization, and to a greater respect for individual Jesuits' career desires. These are essential conditions to the Society's significant survival in the next quarter century. And I have pushed for respect within the Society for the individual's basic American rights, especially those which are habitually violated by superiors: privacy of mail, right to face one's accusers, right of due process, right of appeal. All of these rights have been denied me in this present case.

---

[3] That happened in 1975 with the founding of Matteo Ricci College at Seattle University. It is an "early" college in which students at Seattle Prep (where Jerry taught) and other Seattle Catholic schools begin earning college credits while still in high school, and then proceed to Matteo Ricci College.—PS

I do not say this to be bitter about the Society. I don't want bitterness in my life. I say it simply to push the Society to grant Jesuits their civil rights. I realize respecting these rights makes it slightly more difficult to dispose one's manpower at will, but convenience does not seem important enough a reason to ask men to surrender for life even some of their civil rights.

It is important for you to understand that much of what I have discussed or done is not something I am committed to at all for sure; so much is simply promising possibilities that we need to find the truth about. Everything concerning both sex and psychedelic drugs falls within this category. I have no sure answers, no positions about these things. But I know—from the inside out—how certainly religious and political leaders have no germane answers either, however adamantly they express themselves. I, at least, and others of us, do have relevant experience and some understanding, if not definite answers.

Moral Brinkmanship

What I have tried to describe is my growth as a Jesuit wholly within the ambit the Society chose to educate me in.

This development led me to recognize the actual role of organized religion and to dedicate myself to expanding that role nearer to its real dimensions. In practice, of course, I have tried to carry out my hopes within the Society *as it is now*. This has necessitated a sort of moral brinkmanship.

The risks involved, and the fairly broad restrictions on most of my freedoms, I felt were worth the project: to spend my life helping religion help people.

There were always many solid motives for leaving the Jesuits. But I had wanted, and spent a lot of effort encouraging others, to remain in continuity with what had made us and to transform it from within, rather than simply abandon it to its 19th-century helplessness. I was not a hypocrite, but a reasonable man. It would have been so much easier, and so much more congenial to my character, to have been a purist and told all—with a sort of indelicate honesty, a broadside authenticity. Instead I revealed of myself to each person what each was capable of understanding. For I have really experienced that the best gift I have for anyone is the honest revelation of who I really am. Naturally I made mistakes—many in earlier years, fewer lately. It was this revelation of myself that made this dismissal possible, for no one knows such things about me except for my telling them. As I said, it was a way of living that was a necessary calculated risk. Why it was necessary and why a risk should be clear to you now. Here's how the risk broke.

Civil Wrongs

A couple of months ago I wrote a letter to a younger Jesuit who is a close friend of mine. I tried to prudently reveal what I was going through, but his superior, who opened and read the letter, was disturbed enough by it to send it to the Provincial instead of delivering it to my friend. As the Provincial admitted to me in our fateful interview, there was nothing really problematic about the letter itself. But it led to an "investigation of me and my activities." Father Provincial said it was not enemies but good friends who accused me (!), and certainly from my good friends, trusted friends, I have hid nothing.

But then neither do I believe that any of those I know to be my friends has made these false accusations. Father's informers were widely misinformed about me, or operating on conjecture in place of knowledge. But why I don't know, I just can't understand. And what wasn't false, I felt was generally misunderstood—so completely out of context, half-facts far from home. But certainly the basic fact revealed, that my values are not their values, was true to the core.

Coming out of lunch on Tuesday, May 21st, after 12 years and 257 days in the Jesuits, with 18 days to go till ordination and four days after I sent out our family's 500 invitations, I was stopped by Father Rector and told that the Provincial was flying in from Puerto Rico just to see me. He was in Puerto Rico in conference with the other American Provincials and Father General from Rome. The Rector did not know how or why the Provincial was coming or when he would arrive.

As it happened, it was the worst of days. I was scheduled to take my comprehensive oral exam in systematic theology at 3:15 and my Mass exam at 4:45. I spent the nervous hours waiting by practicing Mass for my exam. With my best friend, Dave Sprague, I said "Mass" and gave him "Communion." I began to feel very apprehensive about the Prov's flying in just to see me. I'd be up in the Northwest in just a few days anyhow, where he could see me with much less éclat.

Being with Dave, I realized deeply how I am good and just another belonging part of what's happening in the Jesuits, the Church, and some areas of American life. I'm not a black sheep or some evil maverick. I felt along my body and through my spirit how I was a sincere, intelligent, dedicated, if not always wise, man. There were simply no legitimate grounds on which anyone could make me feel guilty.

Frightened as I was, I enjoyed the oral exam, discussing with sympathetic professors these very issues I live for. Immediately after the exam, and in the minutes before the next, I was to see Father Provincial.

His first words to me were bitter. "Well, you've turned out to be a Jekyll and Hyde, Jerry." But our discussion was good, the discussion of reasonable, caring men who like and respect each other. Our conclusion was a joint one. I concurred, at the time, that de facto necessities were leaving him no choice. He had to choose between believing my accusers and believing me. He chose to believe my accusers. He refused to believe me, even if I swore on the Bible lying on the desk, which I offered to do.

He refused to believe the testimony of those innocent friends of mine who were included in the false accusations. On the other hand, he would not name my accusers, nor would he permit me to confront them. Moreover, I was to have no right to any sort of a trial or to any appeal to the Society. Father General just that morning in Puerto Rico had personally ratified his decision. On my accusers' word he was dismissing me. Period.

Thirteen Years and Thirteen Minutes

By the end of the interview, Father said I was not a hypocrite, that I was sincere and that the issue was our differing value systems. I appreciated his treating me without contempt or loathing. Coming from a superior that would have made it much harder to keep believing in myself.

I was gone from Alma and the Society within two hours.

From the moment I realized the inevitable, I was peaceful. I am peaceful now (no telling what the residue of my old self-hatred may try to do to me later, but I will fight false guilt with what I know to be true). And I am quietly happy, very happy. Not at all because I am leaving the Society; my commitment to it was as thorough as I knew how, just as it was complex, contoured by the shape of my other commitments as well. I guess I really don't know why I am happy, peaceful.

Certainly in part, though, because my dismissal was a genuine historical confrontation: the Church was typically faithful to its values (whatever I may think of them), but so was I to mine. I have a thing about history. Paul says that all things work together unto good for those who love God; but that's theology—and theology gives meaning to history. History is something else: the most obvious characteristic of its dynamic is precisely that not all good things are coherent or reconcilable. In the relentless measures of space and time, the colliding lawlessness of history crushes the Pollyannas and the logicians, leaving us no recourse but acceptance, hope, healing, hard work, the surd of play, the dance before death.

Perhaps another reason I feel good about myself is that my dismissal is no break in the basic lines of my life. All the important continuities go on— friends, experimental education, that stalking of wisdom that is philosophy, my exploration of the affective domain, the bright pools of this California subculture that intrigue me, and the broader values I love.

I don't so much feel I've been ejected from the Society, as that, like a no-longer needed clay mold, the Society somehow has cracked and fallen away from me. Born free. I guess it's natural. I dislike the arrogant overtone of what I'm feeling; I want to be grateful for what the Society gave me over so many years. I want those of you Jesuits whose lives were closely bound up with mine, and who share my values and the act of creation that our lives together were, and yours still are, to realize how much I believe in you, in your complex role as contemporary Jesuits. I am hoping you will be able to carry out in the Society the development I had dedicated myself to till now: the enlargement of the Society, the Church, and religion for the sake of men around us who suffer. I am with you now not as a Jesuit, but, like always, as I am.

Jerry Swift

Made in the USA
San Bernardino, CA
26 September 2015